Killing an Idea:
Exhuming Say's Law

By Rand McGreal

Dedication

For Robert D. McGreal, MD,

who encouraged me to be analytical.

Preface

This is the second book in the Lost series about the economists who defined the study of economics. This book is an imaginary narrative of a meeting between Jean Baptiste Say and a modern economist in 2013. For the hundred years after his death in 1836, Say's account of economics was considered the gospel. Not until John Maynard Keynes published *The General Theory of Employment, Interest, and Money* was his supply side view of economics challenged. Quotes from Keynes' book are taken from 1997 edition published by Prometheus followed by the page number referenced in this format: (GT p.-xx).

This book reflects Say's views as much as careful speculation allows. Quotes from Say's book, *A Treatise on Political Economy*, are taken from the American Sixth Edition and are referenced by the abbreviation (TOPE loc. xxx) followed by the location number from the e-book version published by Amazon. The events take place in Portland, Oregon over two days in October 2013. Enjoy.

Rand McGreal, June 2014

Seattle, U.S.A.

Table of Contents

Acknowledgement

I want to put in a special thank-you to my Editor Joel David Palmer. He brings a variety of experiences to his editorial work including positions as a research scientist, agricultural engineer, writer, musician, mediator, and big rig truck driver. In his spare time he writes. Recently, he finished *Fugue State: Saddam Dreams*, an Iraq War novel based on Saddam Hussein's final two weeks of freedom. In the work David explores the nature of evil and the possibility of redemption.

As a musician he has released several CDs of ambient, atmospheric, and cinematic instrumental guitar music, and has played on numerous recordings by other artists. Joel makes his home in Seattle.

Killing an Idea:
Exhuming Say's Law

1: Appearances

Have you ever talked to a corpse? It is not uncommon. Many people do at funerals, but I'm meeting one for lunch.

Right now, I'm standing on the corner of Fourth and Burnside in Portland, Oregon—waiting for the light to change—so I can cross over to the corpse world. Not really, but it feels like it. Burnside divides the city into old and new, past and present. I'm standing in the new part, but my meeting is across the street in the old part—with a man who died.

I'm hesitant to go. I know a hell-storm awaits. People have not been kind since his death.

The light changes. I drop off the curb and head north. The drizzly weather on this early October day in the Pacific Northwest casts a proper pall over my meeting.

*****

I should explain. The dead man's name is Jean Baptiste Say (1767-1832). He is, or was, a respected and famous economist. He should be ranked alongside Adam Smith, but he isn't. He advanced economics with his ideas about letting the market set prices, and about the importance of product development. For Say the eighteenth century revolutions in the United States and France heralded a one-hundred-and-eighty degree change in economic leadership. He foresaw how the market system would make the consumer king. He anticipated how top-down control by a handful of royals would succumb to the boiling force of bottom-up consumer pressure. On the eve of the Industrial Revolution, he explained how the engine to drive this economic transformation was industrial production. He explained how business creates societal wealth, in a theory that other economists called Say's Law. Yet today he resides in obscurity.

Say's theory went uncontested until 1936 when a British mathematician, John Maynard Keynes, pushed Say's ideas through a mathematical sieve to test their validity. From his position inside the British government Keynes was desperately seeking a solution to the unemployment created by the Great Depression. When Keynes analyzed the strained contents that came through his testing of Say's ideas, he found evidence supporting his alternative theory of monetary stimulus. Keynes used his analysis to belittle his adversary's ideas about the market, and promote his own economic theory. Keynes became the dominant economist of the twentieth century and Say disappeared. The consequence of Keynes' interpretation of Say's theory was to restore the economic power that governments had lost in the 'freedom' revolutions of the eighteenth century. The royalists overlooked the market power of their citizens in favor of their own opinions about the use of capital. Top down control won out. Keynes used his position inside government to implement his theory. He exploited his prestige as a government official to discredit Say's free market ideas. So here we are today. Say's theory still has virtually no role in the day-to-day management of the world's economies. And Keynes sits on the economic throne.

*****

My trepidation concerns how Say was bashed in the twentieth century. He must hold some resentment. I'm curious how Mr. Say will react to Mr. Keynes' interpretation of his ideas.

My meeting with Say is in one of the oldest buildings in Old Town. Opened as a hotel, today's destination is now a pizza parlor. I know the building well from when I lived in Portland during the 1980s. I'll fill you in with a little history of the restaurant when I get there. It's only a block away now. I am anxious to get inside out of this persistent drizzle.

As I walk this last block, let me briefly introduce myself. My name is Peter Barrie. I live in the Salinas Valley of California. I write and teach economics, specifically about how countries can extract themselves from the devastating effects of too much debt. I'm a not-so-prominent economist, but I have written a book, *Rule of Money*, with a new monetary theory built on the private sector use of debt promulgated by Say and an early 18th century economist named Richard Cantillon. Keynes, Say's main adversary, encouraged the use of debt by the public sector—government. I'm here to learn more about Jean Baptiste Say and his perspective on our use of debt today.

Well, here I am outside Olde Towne Pizza. As I reach for the door handle l feel a slight chill.

In its earlier life as a hotel, the building had once served as a prominent stop for wealthy visitors in the shipping and lumbering trades. As I step into the dark, low-ceilinged space, I head straight for the woodstove across from the entry.

I pause in front of the stove and then, fear freezes me. *I am either meeting a ghost, or someone who has concocted an elaborate put-on. Neither is an enticing situation. I want to meet Say, but I'm questioning the circumstances of my invitation. I'm—afraid of meeting a corpse—afraid of entering a haunted place—afraid of getting entangled in something I don't understand—in a notorious haunt of the unsavory.*

Shaking my head to clear these thoughts, I uncurl my clenched fingers to the stove's warmth, I look around hoping I haven't been observed and refreshing my memory of the place. I came here a couple of times when I visited Portland. A numbers-cruncher needs a refuge. The dark interior of the space recalls the age when candlesticks covered with hundreds of melted wax trails were the only source of light. The large room is not unlike the lower level of an old wooden ship. Heavy timber posts hold up the upper floors, and block a clear view of the interior. Many of the features of the worn hotel remain. The original reception desk has been converted into a bar and a couple of the decorative cast iron columns from the hotel lobby have been left in place. There is comforting reek of garlic, oregano, and beer.

The place feels comfortable now, but memories of its past sends a cool wisp across my shoulder blades, *or am I just chilled?* I know from the hotel's history that many visitors, not unlike me, entered for warmth and comfort over the past 150 years. They set foot through the same door I just closed, anticipating a pleasant evening with new acquaintances. Often, their evenings ended by falling unconscious off a bar stool or meeting the butt end of a pistol. The attentive bar staff quickly helped them to their feet and supported them on a journey down long dark tunnels beneath the hotel that stretched to the port. Conscious or unconscious, these visitors ended up below deck and chained to the gunnels of the clipper ships setting sail for China or Japan. These so-called Shanghai Tunnels were the departure point for many unchosen careers as merchant seamen. *I wonder what fate awaits me.*

Even with the varied history of this old traveler's haunt, I think, I know where I will find Jean Baptiste Say. The restaurant has a resident ghost, Nina, whose afterlife began with a push down an open elevator shaft. I am confident that the tale of a beautiful young working girl's death at the hands of a sanctimonious preacher will draw Say to a seat near where she died. These days Nina floats unseen throughout the restaurant, but near the boarded up shaft is a good spot to get a whiff of her perfume as she drifts about.

The elevator shaft is now a sofa alcove at the rear of the pizza hall. I hate to leave the woodstove, but I shouldn't procrastinate any longer. I walk down the aisle between the tables at the front of the restaurant, to the far back corner. Sure enough, as I get closer to the alcove, I can see two men talking on a Nina influenced loveseat. I approach, scrutinizing their expressions. Quickly, a tall, thin, middle-aged man in a dark business suit focuses his attention on my approach. His deep eyes and straight groomed black eyebrows contrast with his very white face. "Are you Peter?"

"Yes," I answer, reaching my hand out. "Are you Mr. Say?"

"Please, not so formal. I prefer Jean Baptiste or JB," he replies, scanning me with his scrutinizing gaze. "Please meet my new friend, Henry. He is the head chef here."

I reach across the table to the seated Henry and shake his hand, moist from the beer he'd just put down. "Glad to make your acquaintance. I'm Peter Barrie."

"Happy to meet you," the chef says, rising from the couch and wiping his hands on his apron, "I'm Henry Tang. I know you two have a lot to talk about, and I have a kitchen needing a chef, so I'm going to sneak away." Slowly forcing his big body up and out of the petite seat, he stands. Turning back around to Jean Baptiste, he says, "I enjoyed our conversation, JB. I'll prepare that list for you. Give me some warning next time you're headed this way, and I'll make something special for you."

"*Merci beaucoup.* I will be back," Jean Baptiste replies.

He sounds normal. He looks normal. Well, maybe he isn't a ghost. Maybe, the scene is totally staged. I was just as confused when I first met his fellow traveler, Richard Cantillon, six months ago. Eventually, I decided it didn't matter.

Chef Tang passes, blocking the light from the windows, and heads back to the kitchen, I turn to JB. "Nice guy. Did he introduce you to Portland?"

"Oui, he did. He is preparing a list of places he recommends that I see before departing this fine city."

"I hope I'm not late. I wasn't sure exactly what time to arrive."

"Oh, not a problem. I have time under control."

"That's a good skill to possess."

"It is a skill we all acquire late in life."

I sit down at the far end of the couch, turn sideways, and look at Jean Baptiste. He stares back awaiting my questions. I don't immediately fill the silence. I am hurriedly reconsidering the line of questions I planned.

Stumbling over this mental trench of my own making, I say, "I hate to begin with the questions a minute after meeting you for the first time, but how did you find out about me?" *'Begin with questions.' Peter, what are you doing? Get to know the guy! Make some small talk.*

"My good friend Richard Cantillon told me about you. I thought perhaps you could help me, like you helped him," Jean Baptiste explains.

I hesitate a bit before answering. "Thank you for the compliment. But it's Richard who deserves my thanks. He clarified for me the shape of the foundation stones of economics. What kind of assistance can I give you?"

"I need someone to join me in a battle against an economic injustice."

"An economic battle—that's my favorite kind of conflict. Who're we taking on?"

"John Maynard Keynes."

Stunned I consider my response. "Not to be facetious, but might you consider a weaker adversary?"

"There are two of us against the one of him. That squares the odds," says Jean Baptiste with a smirk.

"Right.... You know Keynes doesn't stand alone—he brings with him the entire economic establishment and most of the governments of the western world. Why are you taking on such a daunting task?"

"I want to correct a wrong," he says as his voice pitches skyward, "Excuse me if I get emotional." Jean Baptiste moves to the front edge of the couch. "Keynes broke the first rule of ethical economics by incorrectly restating my views. Then he broke the second rule when he projected outcomes not in agreement with my basic theory. Keynes stated that Say's Law implied that economic slumps were impossible. He did that in the midst of the Great Depression, when millions around the world were looking for employment. You can imagine that made my ideas. My reputation was smeared," Jean Baptiste says, weakly spreading his arms and then quickly dropping them. "Putting words in my mouth about such an important topic was despicable. He and his theories should be stricken from all legitimate economic texts. The man is an unethical menace."

I had wondered how Say would respond to Keynes' characterization of his views. Now I knew. Let the fireworks begin—question answered.

"I would prefer never to hear his name mentioned. I never referred to anything in my theoretical writings or speeches as Say's Law." Say sinks back into the couch, takes a moment to regain his composure, starts to speak, and then pauses again.

I'm speechless. I don't know what to say.

I study Jean Baptiste as he struggles to regain control. "That's a big target you're taking on."

"I know, but the man hurt me deeply. I must restore my name."

"Keynes is dead. How can you get back at the dead?" I ask. *Some irony in that question.*

"What? I am not trying to get back at Keynes! I am trying to restore my reputation. Look at me! Dead or alive is not the issue. What matters is getting the science of economics properly anchored."

This is one animated corpse. Ghost or elaborate put-on, I'm not sure, but if it's a put-on someone has spared no expense. This actor is good. "Okay, you draw a battle line around Keynes and his sycophants. That is a battle I will gladly join. Do you have a battle plan?"

2: Hell-storm

"Keynes has sequestered himself in the most impenetrable of castles—the academic tower of Babble. I want to breach the walls and set a charge that will reduce his ramparts into a pile of stinking rubble. Then I want to enter his crypt and raise an axe over his head, and drive the stout blade into his chest, slicing through his ribs and splitting open his heart like a ripe watermelon!"

"That level of brutality even taken out on a corpse will get into trouble with the authorities."

I consider where next to go. A melodrama is not what I want to hear.

"I get the point. How are we going to take this monster on? How can I help?"

"I need someone to write a treatise explaining Keynes' egregious misrepresentation of my views and to restore my reputation."

"You want me to write an article and correct his misstatement of your theories?"

Oh, Mr. Say, you're imagining the impossible. The academic world will not respond as you expect. They will strike back at the slightest criticism of Keynes. No one wins against him. And there's this other issue: do you even have the arguments to make a case against Keynes?

Jean Baptiste stares at me intently and observes my internal conflict. He continues, "No, I need more than that. I need a complete refutation of Keynes and everything he supports. The man has shoved the earth off its axis with his absurd and ridiculous mischaracterizations of my views. His actions are tantamount to character assassination."

This discussion is going from the impossible to the ridiculous. "Jean Baptiste, you're going a bit overboard. Keynes was stating his view of your theories. He may have misunderstood a point here or there, but I'm sure he didn't intentionally set out to damage your name—he just disagreed with you. This situation sounds a bit like the old joke: What happens when you put three economists in a room? You get four opinions."

"If he wasn't lying, then it was a nationalistic attack!"

I'm not making progress here.

"What do you call it when someone from a rival nation intentionally misrepresents your views, the highly regarded economic theories of the most prominent French economist in an attempt to trivialize and disgrace the economic ideas that sustain a country? I can assure you that the entire French nation was humiliated by his attacks, and the subsequent blind adulation he received from his countrymen. His theories were popularized throughout the world by his British sycophants. They parrot his views because, according to them, he proved that my theory was wrong. But *he* was wrong! He built his reputation by attacking mine! My theory is the correct one. His was an attack on French intellectual thought. Do not deny it!" Jean Baptiste bangs his palms on the arm of the couch not once, but three times.

What am I getting into? I'm not sure the character argument against Keynes is the way to go. How do I handle this? Peter, forget about trying to defuse the situation. You need to get away from this powder keg. "Jean Baptiste, this is a ticklish situation. I don't think I want to get involved."

"Please excuse me, Peter. Please give me a chance. I am so sorry—I let my emotions get the better me. I am usually a rational man.

"Please, let me begin again. His attack has possessed me for almost eighty years. You can understand that. You can understand that the man used me to propel his legacy and to destroy mine. Please help. Please. Please."

Maybe, if I take a few more moments to listen, I can get away without affecting my relationship with Richard Cantillon. I sure hope so. I don't want to screw that up.

"Well, since I drove all the way down here, and I'm hungry, let's at least have lunch. You do eat, don't you?"

"Of course. I need energy to think."

Maybe that's the problem.

"I'll go order, and then we can discuss your proposal, but I think you're going about it in the wrong way. And I'm quite confident I'm not the best person to help you."

"Oh, you are. I am French. I am emotional, but I can go about this in an unemotional way. I should not be speaking on an empty stomach. Let us order some pizza."

"That's a good idea. It's a great day for a hearty lunch. Pizza sounds good. How 'bout a couple of beers to go along with it?"

"*Oui*, I am sure you can see that I need one. I prefer French wine, but a German beer is just fine. It does stretch my endurance, a lunch of Italian food with no wine. Thank you for ordering. I will just sit here and relax."

"Although Oregon has great wine especially *Pinot Noir*, this is not the place to sample it. They specialize in beer. Portland is equally famous for her microbrews. I'll get you something special. Are you allergic to any foods?"

"What does allergic mean?"

"Do any foods give you a churning stomach or a rash?"

"*Non*, I am French. I can eat anything, but I will never say it is good," he says with a sly grin.

"Spicy?"

"Spicy is tolerable."

As I stand to go order at the window, Jean Baptiste reaches for his pipe. "Sorry, but all restaurants here are non-smoking."

"If that is the situation, then I am going to step outside and have a drag while you order."

"Go ahead. I'll meet you back here."

I walk up to the window used for placing orders, pick up a menu, and look for a couple of unique items.

"What can I help you with, sir?" says the young man behind the window.

"I would like four slices: two thin crust BBQ Pulled Pork and two Dragon Ladies also on thin crust. Could you add some anchovies to the Dragon Ladies?"

The young man turns his head and shouts into the kitchen, "Two slices of squealing pork and two DLs with anchovies." To me he says, "What do you want to drink?"

"Let's see. How about two Vanport Pale Ales."

"Great, we'll have that ready for you in twenty minutes."

I walk back to the alcove and wait for Jean Baptiste to return.

When he returns I suggest, "Let's move to a table. We'll have more room to eat." We move just outside the alcove and sit down on two old iron frame chairs painted white.

As we sit down I notice a flowery fragrance. I say, "Our beers will be served shortly. Jean Baptiste, did you smell that perfume?"

"I did notice a weak perfume smell that followed us from the alcove."

"Do you think it's Nina?"

"Peter, you don't believe in that nonsense?" said Jean Baptiste with twinkling eyes and a wry smile.

"There are times when I let down my guard." *Like now, my mysterious friend. Jean Baptiste is putting up the same enigmatic front as*

Richard Cantillon did when I met him in Seattle. Are the two of them ghost conspirators? Or maybe I'm crazy. Instead of traveling to Portland, I should be on a psychiatrist's couch describing these visions. "Mr. Barrie, how many ghost friends do you speak with regularly? Oh, I see. Take eight of these pills a day until the visions disappear."

"Ha, ha, ha!" was the last thing I heard as my psychiatrist disappeared in a puff of white smoke.

After returning and sitting for a moment and running his fingers through his curly black hair, Jean Baptiste says, "I got off on the wrong side of the horse when we first met. Let me begin again. I believe I have a compelling case." I shift uncomfortably in my chair. "Please hear me out," he says quickly. "I may persuade you to reconsider my offer. In the meantime shall we enjoy the day? What kind of pizza did you order?"

Jean Baptiste's new attitude is refreshing, but will it last? Waiting for me to order evidently gave him time to collect his thoughts. I should just enjoy the change for as long as it lasts. Perhaps he was suffering from nicotine withdrawal. "I ordered two slices of the Barbecue Pulled Pork and the Dragon Lady. They're two of the most popular pizzas sold here. I thought they'd give you a taste of Portland."

"The pulled pork will be a treat. What is the Dragon Lady?"

"It's an Italian vegetarian pizza. It has onions, olives, mushrooms, sundried tomatoes, artichoke hearts, and a sprinkling of capers. I asked them to add some anchovies on top."

"That makes my stomach rumble in anticipation. I love the flavor of anchovies—much more appealing to my French palette than harsh Italian sausage!"

"It's going to take about twenty minutes." I look around the pizza parlor and notice the similarities to the Merchant Café in Seattle where I first met Richard Cantillon. Both are in 19th century hotels converted into restaurants. Both have a history of ghost encounters. And both resist any temptation to remodel.

Olde Towne Pizza, like the Merchant Café, is lit by *faux* Tiffany style lamps, a necessary concession to the 21st century. The mixture of round oak tables with carved lion paw legs, and small round white marble top tables with painted cast iron legs, works to take their customers back to the 19th century. *I wonder if it could work in reverse—could people, specifically economists, from the past be transported into the present-day.*

My musing is interrupted by the arrival of our beers.

"Two pale ales for two pale faces. Is that right?"

"You got it, sister," I say in my deepest voice to our attractive waitress. She has exploited her earthy sexual appeal by wrapping a pair of skin-tight jeans around her trim, athletic legs. She wears a short tight black tee that leaves an inch of bare skin exposed above her jeans. A pair of REI hiking boots, an Italian scarf tied around her dark blond hair, and a wristwatch pushed up around her small lean bicep completes the look.

"Ya doin' okay, so far?" she asks.

Jean Baptiste doesn't make a sound. He's in a staring trance.

"Thanks, we're good," I say.

3 : Market Control

As the waitress walks away, it occurs to me this might be a good time to learn more about the relationship between Richard Cantillon, the first famous European economist I met, and my current lunch date.

"Jean Baptiste, I'm curious. When you talk with Richard Cantillon, do you do that telepathically or in person?"

"I communicate with him through feelings. I suspect it is similar to the way the Pope communicates with God. My relationship with Richard is close."

"Are you deeply religious?"

"Every Frenchman has roots in the Catholic Church."

I ask, "In the 18th or 19th century did you and Richard ever meet in Paris?"

"Once in Paris, and a couple of times at other locations."

"Is it possible you were mistaken about the meeting, or that someone arranged a ruse?"

"Deceit and intrigue in Paris? You must be kidding!" he says sarcastically, then calls my bluff. "I suppose it's possible. Do you think I might not be real?"

"Well, that possibility occurred to me," I admit.

"Look at it this way. I'm going to give you some insight into my views, and you can use that information to craft a bestseller and make some money."

"Can you guarantee a bestseller?"

"Can you guarantee a book that deserves to be a bestseller?"

"If I write it, it'll be bestseller worthy!"

"TWO PULLED PORK SLICES AND TWO SLICES OF DRAGON LADY WITH ANCHOVIES."

"Oh, that's our order. Wait here. I'll go get it."

Jean Baptiste's answers are evasive. I'm just as confused as ever. Is this guy real or part of an elaborate ruse? And why would anyone try to deceive me? Could it be my colleagues in the economics world? Possibly. No, that's too farfetched.

I return to the table and set the two platters in the center. "Have you ever had pizza?" I ask.

"*Sacre bleu,* pizza was popular in the 18th century. Naples and Rome were both famous for their pizza. You act like I was born in the Middle Ages."

Jean Baptiste reaches for a slice of pizza and takes a bite. "Hmm, that is spicy, but delicious."

"Oops, I forgot to tell you about the jalapeno peppers. Those green pieces spread across the top of the pizza are jalapeno, a hot pepper from Mexico. Is it too hot for you?"

"No, no, it's fine. I like the intense flavor."

"If I write about you and Keynes, should I describe your conflict as 'sharp as a jalapeno?'"

"You can describe me as 'sharp as a jalapeno', and Keynes as 'honest as a gold prospector giving directions to his claim'."

"I can't picture you and Keynes enjoying a slice of pizza and a beer."

"It would be a picture of contrasts. One dignified cultured Frenchmen and one insipid Englishman. I can see by your expression you want me to quell my anger at Keynes. Taking the high road, let me say that I have a fundamental difference of opinion with Keynes about how to encourage economic growth. Keynes believed government agencies should be empowered to manipulate the economy. I believe the best control of the economy is the market. Government versus market control is the heart of our differences. I believe the market cannot be wisely manipulated by government policy. Anyone promoting government control is devious."

"Okay, but a difference of opinion over state control and market control is not that big a deal. Why all the animosity?"

"He libeled me. He launched his economic career through false statements about my theories. I have every right to be offended."

"Okay, I understand your position. Can you just lay out the particulars so I can get a clearer picture?"

"You just made my first point: we came at economics from different perspectives. Keynes' father was an economics teacher, and Keynes spent most of his career in the civil service or doing projects for the state. He was a progeny of the government sector. He never worked in the business sector. My life, on the other hand, was in the business sector. After my education, I went to work for a merchant in London. Then I was in the insurance industry for a couple of years, and next I worked as a publisher of the 'radical' views of Adam Smith. I finally found my place in society as a cotton industrialist. Unlike Keynes I did not write about economics to justify a proper role for government in the financial system, but to explain to ordinary citizens how the economy works and to help maximize business productivity, create employment, and build wealth."

This is a real discussion! Maybe there is hope for my angry companion. "Now we're making progress. Please go on."

"So we have two men with different ideas about what economics should be. I think legislatures should write laws and regulations that encourage business, and Keynes thought government can encourage economic growth through monetary controls. In other words, Keynes wanted top-down state control, and I want bottom-up market control with minimal governmental interference."

I'd caught a brief glimpse of an early spring, but now I feel a cool wisp emanate from the frozen soul of my passionate lunch partner. "I get the picture. You have one undercover agent working for the government and one for the business sector. Does it surprise you that you two would not find common ground? But taking shots at him is probably unnecessary and unproductive."

"Peter, his was a one-sided duel. I was dead."

"Oh, yeah, Keynes did have that advantage."

As I speak, I notice that the couple at the table next to us is saying very little—unusual behavior for a pizza parlor. Just as Jean Baptiste begins to speak again the women reaches up and wraps a wayward strand of hair behind her ear. She's wearing bright red fingernail polish, peculiar for Portlandia—green or sunset purple polish, or none at all, would be more typical here.

Are they listening to us?

Jean Baptiste says, "I disagree with Keynes about most aspects of economics. We even had different objectives in our study of economics. I saw the objective of economics as creating a system to supply products and services. Keynes saw economics as a system to adjust output and employment. Consequently, we ended up formulating theories that were different. As I explained in my *Treatise* (TOPE loc. 55-556), theory is the 'knowledge of the laws that connect effects with their causes.' To simplify the difference between us, Keynes was looking for the cause of high employment and I was looking for the cause of high national wealth."

"From a practical standpoint the result should be the same," I say.

"I agree. It was our approaches to the problem that differed. I look at the world from the perspective of an entrepreneur. What makes an entrepreneur start or expand a business? Keynes looked at what a national government could do to move the economy upward."

"I understand that difference in approach, but the outcome is the same so why does it matter?"

"It doesn't matter if we both reach the same destination. But we took different paths and one of us did not complete the journey; consequently we ended up at different destinations."

"I think you set me up. Who got off track?"

"Keynes missed a couple of his connections. He sought a model of the economic universe like that which Galileo discovered for the planets. Keynes thought there were certain fixed patterns in a robust economy and other patterns in a slumping economy. For instance, in a robust economy demand is high and unemployment low, while the opposite occurs in a slumping economy. We agreed about those observations, but differed on how to maintain a boom or escape a slump."

Jean Baptiste rubs his index finger across his lower lip a couple of times then says, "Keynes thought total spending was the Sun in our economic solar system. Like the Sun, total spending provided the energy for the economy to thrive. Energy determined whether a planet was a frozen orb like Pluto or a green productive planet like Earth. I agree with Keynes that a large stable heat source is essential to the economy, but throwing another log into the Sun's furnace is less effective than lighting a fire in one's own hearth. Writing laws to enable more logging is more effective than hiring people to count the number of cold cottages.

"Another place where Keynes and I drift apart is in reference to Earth's Moon. Keynes thought the pull from of the Moon, the government in this analogy, was essential to keep the Earth in a stable orbit. He considered the Moon like a wise old uncle giving direction to the big clumsy kid in the family. I feel the Moon's role was inconsequential, and negative when it moved to block the Sun. Keynes felt that the relative position of the two spheres determined employment and economic growth on Earth. I believed the only significant activity is what happens on Earth and in the marketplace. If conditions are optimal, growth will be vigorous; if not, then adjustments need to be made on Earth in the business environment. Lunar effects and man-in-the-Moon economics are just fables."

He pulled at the dangling lobes of his ears and continued, "Before I get ahead of myself let me emphasize what I just said. The market should be left to set the employment level for the economic conditions. This approach implies that the right action for a legislative body is to modify the economic conditions so employment can be higher. Keynes' approach, dictating instead of listening, tries to force employment higher when conditions may not warrant higher employment. Peter, like in the Great Recession, the Keynesians forced interest rates lower to encourage more job creation, but nothing happened. Why? The conditions were not right. No entrepreneur saw an opportunity for new business in the slumping economy. The right economic strategy is to open new avenues for permanent job creation. This is what happened. Adoption of oil fracking created millions of jobs. Expanding social media created millions more as it made advertising more personal. No government action created these jobs."

"Well put, you're leading," I acknowledged.

"Let me reiterate, my disagreement with Keynes is not that much about goals or the components to adjust, but how to go about it. The question is who should be king. I say the market and Keynes says the government. It's like two mechanics working to make a ship travel faster.

Keynes wants to replace the captain, and I want to modify the rigging."

I better resign myself to the fact that the barbs will never cease. The couple at the next table put their heads together and mutter something, then straighten up as if they had choreographed their move. *They aren't going to let us overhear their conversation.*

"I am a big fan of system improvements," I say.

"Fan, what does that mean?"

"A sympathizer, a dedicated disciple."

"It is a new word to me."

I leaned toward Jean Baptiste and spoke quietly. "I forgot that you're from the nineteenth century. But that brings up a question. How do you know so much about Keynes? Wasn't he born fifty years after your death?"

"Correct, fifty years is a short time when you stop counting."

I notice that our lunch companions are preparing to leave. *Is it because I leaned in? Did I blow their cover? Or is it a coincidence?* The man stands up; he's wearing all black. His ensemble includes black pants, a skin-tight V-neck sweater, and black leather jacket. His black hair is cut so short it might be a tattoo. He has a black goatee, a sharp thin nose, straight reed-like eyebrows, and slit eyes. He looks like Snidely Whiplash from the Rocky and Bullwinkle show, but without the parrot beak.

His companion gathers her purse of quilted black leather with a jewel at each intersection of the harlequin stitching pattern. She swings her legs out from under the table to reveal black patent leather platform shoes and black tights around her stick-like legs. She grabs her black leather jacket from the seat of the chair next to her. After slipping gracefully into her jacket, she wraps a gray patterned scarf over her head, pulls it down around her ears and under her chin to conceal her childlike crown, tiny flat ears, and most of her short-cropped auburn hair. Her large round penetrating eyes look directly at me as they depart. The black widow and her evil companion disappear without arousing Jean Baptiste's interest.

4: Market vs. Government

"Jean Baptiste, I am a little confused about how you know so much about the theories of an economist who wrote a hundred years after you died."

"Unlike your good friend Richard Cantillon, I prefer to be on the cutting edge of the future. I spend all of my time in the present. Richard prefers the 18th century. I prefer the 21st century."

"That explains your confidence in talking about Keynes, but how did you find out about him?"

"I have read his book and many of his speeches. I have a library card from the *Bibliothèque Nationale* in Paris. I do not go to work every day or watch TV, but I am aware of what is going on in the world and I am well read."

"Have you spoken to any modern economists?"

"You are the first. I have always been afraid of being exposed."

So, Mr. Say, are you a ghost, a time-traveler, or a fake trying to deceive me? Are the man and woman in black your compatriots, ready to step in if the ruse is detected?

"Richard assured me that you would be respectful and, more significantly, discrete."

Pausing to check myself before responding, "I will certainly try to be."

"Peter, do you think you can explain that Keynes' conclusions are wrong?"

The question interrupts my ghost speculation. I turn to face Jean Baptiste directly and not moving an eyelash consider my response. After a moment, "I think you have logic and common sense on your side, but that will not be enough to convince most people. You need to prove Keynes is wrong. It is not enough to prove his criticism of you is unfounded."

"That is why I need your help, Peter."

"Proving Keynes is wrong is not that simple."

"I have a feeling you know how to do it."

"I can assure you that I don't know how. You need to give me more. I get it that you and

Keynes had different viewpoints. I can appreciate that Keynes may have created his theory to justify a larger role for the financial bureaucracy in government. But accusations aren't going to take you very far. You need to prove that Keynes libeled you to further his theory, and then prove his theory is incorrect."

Jean Baptiste stares at me with squinting eyes. He began slowly, "Let me give you a little perspective on my history. My contemporaries overthrew Louis XIV, the symbol of extravagant government. We beheaded the monarchy in France once and forever. We created conditions for the middle class to flourish, and put an end to domestic slavery. We did that despite personal and financial risk to ourselves, for the good of our country. We did not do it for personal glory, but for the glory of our country."

"I agree, you accomplished a lot after the French Revolution, but you also allowed Napoleon to rise to power."

"Granted, but is it fair to criticize a new system when it is in its infancy? Remember, when your middle class was emerging your country you allowed Andrew Carnegie, J.P. Morgan, John D. Rockefeller, and Cornelius Vanderbilt to subvert the rules of business."

"I suppose that's fair. No new system works smoothly at start-up, but I still don't understand the venom you're spewing at Keynes."

Jean Baptiste strokes his goatee. "Why am I still striking at Keynes, because he took my supply theory of growth and dismissed it without proving it was wrong. Dismissal is significant when the person doxing sets the curriculum for the study of Economics. Next, he belittled product making and replaced the product with the shopping bag. Finally, he attacked my theory as not only wrong but ridiculous when he said: *'Say's Law, that the aggregate demand price of output as a whole is equal to its aggregate supply price for all volumes of output, is equivalent to the proposition that there is no obstacle to full employment.'* (GT p.-26) Does that make sense to you?"

"It's a bit vague."

"A bit vague? It is a meaningless corruption of the English language and a misstatement of my views! I never called anything Say's Law, nor said anything about a balance between aggregate supply and aggregate demand! No obstacle to full employment? I would never declare that! Ridiculous! It was just a simplification to belittle me and so poorly stated as to be unassailable. Think about it. How would manufacturers know enough about consumer demand to perfectly balance supply and demand? It is absurd."

"Okay. Okay, I'm with you, but how am I going to refute his charge?"

"Just tell the truth."

"That's the issue. What's the truth?"

"This is not nautical engineering! It is simple banking science. Just like you showed in your *Rule of Money* book, banks make money out of nothing through wise lending. By 'nothing', you meant that banks create assets with only a promise by the borrower to repay the loan. The economy grows every time a bank lends to a new business."

"You read my book?"

"I read all of them. Your idea about the necessity that money be earned intrigued me, so I asked Richard to set up this meeting."

"Well, thank you. I am honored."

"Do you realize you may have discovered the Achilles' heel in Keynes' thinking? Keynes thought governments could just print money, and that this would stimulate the economy. You proved money does not matter. It is new businesses that grows the economy. Keynes' idea of government spending is like a debtor borrowing more to pay off his debts. It doesn't make the debtor solvent or add to the wealth of the nation, and it doesn't make the debtor rich."

"Good description. People will understand your point. Do you oppose all government intervention into the economy?"

"*Oui,* and I would like to see some of these government officials driven through the streets in prison carts and publicly humiliated."

"That's a vision! What exactly is your disagreement with Keynes? Is it about the damage he did to people and countries through the policies he advocated?"

"Correct, and let the punishment match the crime. His clever deception of political leadership resulted in debt being cavalierly accumulated. Promotion of this approach by Keynes has led the 20th century to the brink of financial Armageddon."

"What do you think his punishment should be?"

"That is for you and the living to decide. I just want you to make a compelling case, so the children that now fill the school yards around the world will not be forced to work long hours to pay off the debts of the Keynesians."

"Let's backtrack a second. From a practical standpoint, don't you agree with Keynes that the supply price equals the demand price? That there is an equilibrium point." I ask.

"Not at all. The farmer wants a high price and the grocer wants a low price. The supply price and the demand price are never equal in the beginning. It is only when the final transaction price is agreed upon by both parties that they are equal. Changes in the market move this price day-by-day, minute-by-minute. That is an unstable surface to make a foundation of economics."

"So Keynes' premise about his so-called Say's Law is incorrect, and if his premise is wrong, then his conclusion must be wrong."

"*Oui*, employment is not a function of prices. Employment rises and falls with the number of people employed, not the cost of products. Total employment is related to market size. In most economic slumps, people and companies take shelter, they reduce their risk. Why, because the market deflates. When companies reduce the quantity of their offerings to a few basics, the economy and employment shrinks. Demand does not change, but people stop buying, because they are frightened and scrutinize every purchase."

"Oh, I see—Keynes wanted to relate employment to the amount of money people have to spend and you are saying employment is related to how willing people are to spend."

"Peter, you are jumping ahead. Keynes stated that Say's Law means that economic slumps are impossible. What I am really saying is that human attitudes can change and cause people to become cautious. It is not about the quantity of money in the system as Keynes suggested. When people get cautious they spend less and the economy slumps.

"Why do people suddenly change their perceptions of the future? Government is usually the culprit. In the 1930s when Keynes was trying to come up with a solution for unemployment, government was all-powerful throughout the world. Governments passed tariffs, subsidized favored industries, raised taxes, restricted money flow, and erected barriers to trade in an effort to assert control over the market. When the United States passed the Smoot Hawley Tariff in 1929 international trade slumped 50% as countries retaliated. Instead, their actions unsettled business and made conditions difficult for business and therefore, employment growth."

Jean Baptiste asked for support from his invisible army of followers with open questioning hand gestures as he continued, "Did Keynes tell governments to stop their damaging policies? No, he did not! Rather, he chose to attack an innocent French economist with the venom of an incumbent politician attacking a first time opponent, with lies and exaggeration.

"Keynes accused me of arguing that full employment was inevitable, and that slumps were impossible. Quite the opposite, I recognized that government interference, trade imbalances, entrepreneurial variance, the supply of gold, and business competition all contribute to a bumpy growth pattern. Instead of declaring slumps impossible, I declare them inevitable."

I'm stunned by the strength of his counterattack against Keynes. This is a persuasive and impressive display of knowledge. But how does he know these things?

"Ah, ha! Peter, have I convinced you to help me?"

"Well, I'm on your side, but I don't know if proving that Keynes' General Theory is based on flawed assumptions will change the superstar reputation of the man."

Chef Tang walked around the corner and approaches our table. "Excuse me, guys, can I interrupt you for a moment? JB, here's the list I promised. If you two are touring our city and discussing economics, do you mind if my daughter joins you? She's an economics student and would treasure the experience of listening to you two talk about her field of study." He tears a sheet from an old yellow pad that looks like it has spent a lifetime in the kitchen and hands it to JB.

"Thank you, I would be delighted to have your daughter join us." Jean Baptiste looks through the list and then turns his head up toward the chef. "I am going to try and get to most of these places in the next couple of days. I also intend to take advantage of your offer of a special Korean meal."

"I suggest you start your tour at the Lan Su Chinese Garden just a block away. Thank you for allowing my granddaughter to accompany you. She can meet you there. Sorry for the interruption. Give me a call a couple days ahead of when you want that special dinner, and I'll get things together. Well, I'll let you guys finish your conversation and plan your day. I hope you enjoyed your lunch. I'll tell my daughter to meet you in the Garden."

"Lunch was great. Thanks," Jean Baptiste and I say in unison.

"All right, enjoy your tour." Chef Tang takes Jean Baptiste's hand, gives it a hearty shake, and pats my shoulder as he passes by on his way to the kitchen.

"That was thoughtful of him," I say.

"I met him just an hour ago, and I feel like he is already a good friend."

"So, you're planning to be here a couple of days?"

"*Oui*, I want to explore the city before returning to Europe."

"In that case, we should finish here and go explore. Let's look at the list and chart our afternoon."

"Great idea."

"I lived here in Portland twenty years ago. There have been many changes, but I'd bet many of the highlights are the same."

Quickly glancing at the list, I say, "I'm right. So we start at the Lan Su Chinese Garden. That's a fabulous place. We can continue our conversation as we meander through the garden."

"Give me a minute. I have my beer to finish, and I need a smoke."

"Another smoke?"

"*Oui*, but I will light up outside and take a drag as we walk to this garden."

"Go ahead, finish your beer and we'll depart when you're ready."

After a few moments, Jean Baptiste says he is ready to go. We slowly head toward the Lan Su Chinese Garden, Jean Baptiste puffing away. He smokes in the French style, exhaling through his mouth and inhaling through his nose. A steady stream of poisonous gas exits his mouth and is immediately sucked in the dual orifices of his nose.

5: Employment Factors

As we cross the street to enter the garden, I give Jean Baptiste a prelude, "The Lan Su Chinese Garden is a collaboration between Portland and her sister city, Suzhou in Jiangsu province of China. The Garden is based on the classical gardens of Suzhou constructed by wealthy civil servants in the 16th century during the Ming dynasty. Some historians regard the Ming dynasty as the best example of a period of government managed social and economic stability."

Intrigued, Jean Baptiste asks, "What caused the dynasty to collapse?"

"A number of things, but one major factor was a requirement that taxes be paid in silver even though commercial transactions used copper coins. When the value of silver spiked relative to copper, many farmers and merchants went bankrupt."

"Taxes strike again. People forget that high taxes destroyed every major civilization from the Egyptians to the Romans, as well as the British Empire's control over the American colonies."

"That was a good thing, wasn't it?"

"Only, if you were an American."

After crossing the street we enter the entry courtyard to the Lan Su Chinese Garden. Jean Baptiste lowers his head as he looks at the arrangement of stones laid in the tiles of the courtyard.

Noticing, I comment, "The Chinese are masters of stone in the landscape. It is one of the four elements of Chinese garden design: stone, water, plantings, and architecture. If you look closely at the paving stones, you will notice many turned on edge. The stones are arranged that way to stimulate the sense of touch in your feet as you walk. Chinese gardens are about activating your senses."

"It is a different design approach from our French gardens."

"Is this the first Asian garden you have visited?"

"*Oui*. I've seen illustrations on vases and in paintings, but it is hard to appreciate the style until you actually walk through one."

"European gardens are about space being created through plantings," I point out, "while Asian gardens are less about the plantings and more about molding all the elements into one harmonious whole."

"It is enlightening to see how our different viewpoints are expressed even in garden design," Jean Baptiste notes. "The Chinese garden slowly unfolds as you follow the path. The garden designer leads you along to each view, past an overlook to observe the fish, beneath a tree, or past a group of peonies. It is a deliberate path to appreciation and understanding."

"Then there is the European garden model of broad avenues bordered by trees that often end at a vanishing point on the horizon. That difference must convey some meaning," I offer.

"French gardens are about royal processions or military parades. The gardens are settings for the pageantry of the royal life. There is no contemplation of the connection between man and nature. It is about the wealth and the beauty of the upper classes. Our gardens are like the red carpet at a movie premiere—a stage for the elite to parade."

I point out, "The European garden model molds trees and plants into a form that suits human uses. It is about control. All the trees are formed into a long line along a roadway. Hedges are planted on boundary lines to reinforce property rights. The heavy hand of man rules. It is a very Keynesian approach."

"Well said, even the forest is made to toe to the dictates of man. It is about power, because the beauty of nature cannot be improved. Likewise, the efficiency of the market cannot be improved with the power of the state."

Our conversation had carried us through the Chrysanthemum Gate onto a view of the central pond and next to the Hall of the Brocade Clouds. As the self-appointed guide I said, "This is a traditional setting for homeowners to meet their guests. The main room offers some of the best views of the overall garden—in this case a series of pond views through a row of lattice windows. The views often extend beyond the limits of the garden and may include trees or mountains outside the garden walls.

"See those rocks on the other side of the pond? They all came from China. Fifty tons, if my memory is working. They came from a famous lake near Suzhou: Lake Tai. The rocks were collected beneath the water surface from a limestone formation that erodes in the acidic waters of the lake. The acid burns holes in the rock, forming them into twisted tortured shapes. The result is often a pleasing sculptural piece."

Jean Baptiste walks over to the windows and stood gazing at the water with his arms crossed on his chest like a professor observing a student's work at the chalkboard.

I looked out on the pond and at the islands of lilies with the last blooms of summer still rising above the waters' skin.

"This is what I needed," muttered Jean Baptiste.

Out of the corner of my eye I notice the couple from Olde Towne Pizza walking into a building on the other side of the pond. *Why are they here? Why am I paranoid?*

They disappear into the pavilion, and I turn to see Jean Baptiste approaching.

"Peter, did you ever make the observation that Chinese gardens have multiple points of view? The arrangement of buildings and paths allows you to come upon a new view at each turn. That is quite different from French gardens that have one dramatic perspective to compel your attention. Our gardens are designed with control and precision in mind and here the Chinese have sought to capture many visions of nature. The Chinese seem to want the viewer to explore and we, French want the artist to direct the viewer."

"Yes, it is one of the differences between Western and Eastern art and one of the underlying principles of Chinese garden design."

"Educate me. What is the principle?"

"The garden is laid out as a series of scenes. It is not meant to be seen all at once. The design aesthetic tries to replicate the natural world as much as possible. So the designers try to capture the views one sees on a walk in a natural setting. The garden is designed to mirror a stroll down a woodland path where you come upon a sequence of unexpected views. The garden designers conceal views and plan the layout to surprise and delight the visitor."

With a contented smile on his face Jean Baptiste says, "As I was standing looking at the pond I realized garden design is a metaphor for the difference between my approach to economics and the one Keynes used. Keynes applied a model to the natural world, and I use the natural world to direct us down the economic path to prosperity."

"You're an Asian man masquerading as a Frenchmen."

Paying no attention to me, Jean Baptiste continued, "Like French garden designers, Keynes created a strong axis in his economic landscape and arranged his garden around a simple perspective. Everything derived in his General Theory is from the IS/LM formula, his mathematical model. All the conclusions he reached about investment and employment are from his theory of why entrepreneurs hire labor and make investments. He is a one-trick pony."

"An intriguing thought. That seems to make him vulnerable with one large caveat—if you can show how the IS/LM model is incorrect. The remainder of his theory would then be invalid. I'm going to need your help with that."

"My dear American friend, you shall have it."

"You know," I say, "the IS/LM model is considered the economic equivalent of Einstein's theory of relativity."

"Who is Einstein?"

"Oh, yeah, I guess you don't know everything that happened after your death."

"From an economic standpoint I am quite knowledgeable, but outside my field I am lost."

"Einstein and his theory of relativity is a topic for another day."

"Good. I would like to concentrate on Keynes. Here is another garden metaphor you might put in your new book. You can no more make a model of how a garden will grow after a drought than how the economy will perform after an economic collapse. The fertility of the seeds for regrowth is too variable to predict consistently. Keynes' reliance on models suggests his theories are more prophecy than common sense economics. Keynes' theories amount to asserting that when he came upon an unexplored forest grove, he could use his models to predict its character, without ever taking a step inside, based on the previous forests he had visited."

"I see your point. Keynes imbued his models with predictive powers that may be invalid and unnecessary. He could just as well have walked into the forest and observed what died in the drought and what is struggling, then replant, fertilize, and open the tree canopy to let in more light."

"*Oui. Monsieur*, you are making steady progress."

"Thank you, thank you. I am taking note of these observations, so keep it coming. Let's continue our walk."

We turn a corner and walk along the pond's edge. In the water are large white carp with orange and black splotches, attracted by our shadows. We cross under a covered walkway and stroll along the water's edge until we reach the Fish Pavilion.

"I have seen these fish illustrated in Chinese prints. What kind are they?" asks Jean Baptiste.

"They're Koi. Koi is a Japanese word for carp. I don't know the Chinese word, but fishkeeping moved to Japan from China, so the word may be the same. In both cultures, fish are raised in ponds for eating and for the pleasure of watching them. Fish aquaculture is more than two thousand years old in China."

"Many French households keep fish in ponds for eating. The fish are caught wild in a nearby lake or stream. A fish farmer would take his catch home and store them in a man-made pond until the household wanted to cook them."

At the Fish Pavilion, I tell Jean Baptiste the popular story of how the building got its name. "Two Chinese philosophers were watching fish in a garden pond. The first philosopher commented that he was quite surprised at how happy the fish were. The second philosopher stated, 'You are not a fish. How do you know they are happy?' The first philosopher answered, 'You are not me. How do you know I don't know the fish are happy?' This is the same as the dilemma Keynes faced. How did he know whether people would respond as he predicted in his model? Three times people failed to respond as his model indicated, in the 1930s, the 1980s, and most recently in the years 2008 to 2012."

"What do you mean, people failed to respond?"

"Oh, just that when the government lowered interest rates people did not take out new loans. Or that when the government created more funds for borrowing, businesses did not expand and hire more employees as he predicted."

"State that fact in this new book you are considering—you are still considering it?"

"I am considering it, but I still don't see a high enough economic bridge to span the theoretical torrents of Keynes and his allies."

"Look more closely—you should see some high spans soon. Has anyone ever mentioned that you are a hard case?"

"Not a soul...ever!" I say with a laugh.

Our conversation carries us to a resting spot on the railing of the Lounge House. In this sort of building, traditionally, the family would gather in the evening to listen to music, enjoy painting, or play games such as mahjong together.

Farther down the path we come to an attractive loggia hanging out over the water. We stop for a view directly across the great pond to the western side of the garden and a good view of the pavilion located in the middle of the water. I notice the black widow and her companion, partially hidden inside the floating Teahouse, gazing at us.

"Look across to the pavilion on the water," I say in a low voice, gesturing with my eyes. "Are those the two people who sat across from us at lunch?"

Jean Baptiste slowly raises his gaze from the water and scans the northern edge of the pond, "*Oui*, it looks like they are talking in earnest about something. I saw them earlier, looking in our direction."

"I don't want to be paranoid, but those two bother me. Can you think of any reason they might be following us?"

"*Non.*"

"Well, I'm probably making something out of nothing. Let's just be careful about who overhears us. Come, follow me to the Scholar's Study. It's just ahead. Let's go see if Chinese economists had it better than we do."

"Were there Chinese economists?"

"Oh yes. The first person now recognized as an economist was Chinese, Tao Zhugong, from the fifth century BC. He lived in an area of China not far from where this type of scholar garden compound developed. And he was a merchant, so he may have lived in a house very similar to this one. Remember the garden mountain of white limestone in the corner of the pond? The stones from Lake Tai? Many people believe that Tao Zhugong still rows the fishing waters of that lake."

"A ghost with a mind still wandering about in the world. In that case, I must see his study."

6: Keynes Makes an Error

Walking past a large moon gate, we turn into the alcove concealing the entrance to the Scholar's Study and push open the tall, heavy door. As the view of the interior appears, we are struck by the height of the room and the elaborate woodwork that trims the walls. It is a space defined by the dark wood trim, bright open lattice windows, and a strong sense of solemnity. I walk over to the desk of the scholar. It is three or four inches higher than a typical European desk.

I observe, "It looks like the scholar worked standing up."

Jean Baptiste walks toward the desk in the middle of the room, pausing at one of the room's two chairs. He rubs his hand down the back and across an arm of one of the chairs, tracing the gentle curve of the bent wood. "They read sitting down, it seems. Or perhaps these chairs were intended only for visitors."

Looking around I inquire, "With all this space, do you think he taught students while standing behind his desk?"

"That seems logical, or possibly a gaggle of long-necked courtesans lay on cushions while listening to the great master read sex poetry."

"Oh, the great French mind never travels far from the boudoir."

"I think I have gained a greater appreciation for the Chinese scholar and his burdens!"

"Dare I ask what those might be?"

"Certainly, one of his challenges was satisfying a roomful of giggling courtesans with poetry."

"I am gaining a greater appreciation for the difference between you and Keynes."

"No call for that!"

"Let's see what a great scholar kept on his desk. Although this tabletop is not a desk in the Western sense; lacking drawers, it's more of a work surface. I assume that was to accommodate scrolls and large sheets of paper for drawing."

"Peter, you must be right. Calligraphy is more painting than writing in our sense of the word."

"Look here: the 'Four Friends of the Study'."

"Who are they?"

"The 'Four Friends of the Study' are brushes, ink stick, paper, and ink stone. They are the tools of the scholar. Before you ask: yes, I have taken a couple of Asian art classes."

Jean Baptiste picks up a round stone from the desktop and turns it over. "I am happy that you can explain what these objects are."

"You're holding the ink stone. I think you should put it down. We're supposed to look and not touch."

"Oh, pardon! Excusez-moi!"

"No problem. The ink stone works with this pressed ink stick." I reach across the desk to indicate a six-inch long, thin black object with a pattern of chrysanthemums pressed into its surface. "The ink stick is hard, but when rubbed on the ink stone sheds a dusting of ink powder. The scholar then drips water from this small depression on the ink stone to create the ink slurry.

"The ink stone is for mixing the ink to the right consistency. If you look carefully you will see the top is flattened and carved to resemble a lakeshore, with an edge line similar to a shoreline. The raised edge keeps the ink from running off."

"Ingenious."

"The scholar adds ink dust and water to create the slurry with a certain consistency for his painting subject. Once he is satisfied with the slurry, he picks up some ink on his brush and makes a mark on his paper representing, for instance, a bamboo leaf."

"*Merci beaucoup.* Knowing the artist's tools adds a level to my appreciation of Asian calligraphy and ink painting."

"I shouldn't emphasize painting and calligraphy too much, though, because often a Scholar's Study was used as a study hall to learn the texts needed to enter government service, which was the most desired career path in China. A room like this is where the man of the house read the classics and studied for the grueling examination process of qualifying for civil service, but it is also a place where creativity was encouraged. See those objects stored over there?" I point to the shelves against the far wall. "Each was chosen to stimulate creativity."

"Quite different from the European model where loyalty and conformity are the admired traits of civil servants," says Jean Baptiste.

"Yes," I say, "creativity is not a sought after trait of civil servants in this country, either. But it sure is in the business sector. It's richly rewarded in the commercial world."

"It is enlightening that innovation plays such a role in the modern world, and yet Keynes barely mentions it in his General Theory. In his commentary about entrepreneurs he did not recognize them as innovators, but assigned to them the trait of running businesses based on how much they could earn from each new employee."

"Isn't that idea one of the factors in Keynes' theory about employment?"

"Correct. He believed that entrepreneurs only hired employees when additional profit could be earned from the new employee."

"That sounds like a very naïve understanding of the complexities of business. Are you saying he did not understand the factors of employment?"

"*Oui*, and his assumption that the supply of products is based solely on the demand for products is untrue. Manufacturers often produce more than the market demands; they do it to offer lower priced products in the hope that this will induce additional demand. And there are many other factors that complicate a simple supply and demand model for business.

"For one, consider inventory. Business always produces an excess—we call this inventory. Companies produce inventory to fill unexpected orders with products on hand. Inventory is also useful to refill orders that are lost in shipping or stolen or damaged. Why is this significant? Inventory is an important business activity and it requires borrowed funds to maintain necessary levels. This borrowing expands the money supply and creates a repetitive, though under-appreciated, lending business for banks. In a surging market, companies carry increased inventory because products turn over more quickly. Keynes' model does not address these aspects.

"Keynes' ignorance of business operations makes his analysis of economic forces questionable. Peter, if you ever lose your self-control and choose to write a book about Keynes, you should expose that weakness."

"Now that I think about it," I say, "the derivation of the IS line in his employment model does make one uncomfortable. His assumption that entrepreneurs only hire new employees based on the profit earned from each employee is a 19th century class fallacy.

"One of the last things business people consider when evaluating a new commercial opportunity is calculate labor costs. First of all, this is because it is difficult to calculate labor costs upfront. Before adding labor costs to all the other costs, an entrepreneur must figure out the size of the market, competition, potential market share, selling volume, selling price, and factory floor layout.

"Entrepreneurs begin by adding up manufacturing costs: raw materials, equipment, depreciation, power, land, building, borrowing, packaging, shipping, marketing, and taxes. Then they begin to calculate labor costs. Although labor is a significant cost and cannot be overlooked, it is also an easy cost to calculate. Most entrepreneurs use the cost of labor from other firms that provide the same or similar products."

"I get that. So why do you think Keynes used the amount of money a businessperson makes per employee to create the 'I' line, the investment line in his employment model?"

"My American friend, I can only assume it is because he did not understand business. There is no other explanation. Can you image a Spanish farmer, after tasting his first bland artichoke from Egypt, deciding to raise them because he had read Keynes and determined he could make at least the normal profit he earned on his orange-picking labor? The farmer might compare the cost of artichoke picking without a ladder versus the cost of orange picking from a ladder and then, following Keynes' logic, replace his orange grove with artichoke bushes.

"Of course, this is absurd. What might happen instead is that the farmer would take artichoke samples to his local marketplace to assess consumer interest. Next he would survey his regular customers to see how much they would pay for the new fruit. Then he could evaluate spoilage, consider insect infestations and do some test growing. Keynes's naïve assumptions about business makes interest rates the penultimate reason entrepreneurs invest (GT p.-27-28).

"So ultimately interest rates determine how many people a segment of the economy employs. Am I right about that?"

"Oui, Monsieur."

"Investment is the supply line in a typical supply and demand graph. So using Keynes' logic, if the entrepreneur makes no profit on his employees he will employ zero people. Keynes assumed that as the profit per employee grew, the entrepreneur would hire more and more people (GT p.-24-25). So the Investment line increases or climbs to the right on the graph as the total profit grows."

"Oui, Monsieur."

"Now bear with me," I say. "In Keynes' model the Investment line intersects the Demand line. Demand can be simplified as the amount of money people have available to purchase the products being produced. So if the product is, say, artichokes, and people purchase $1,000 worth of the fruit in a certain community, the Investment line intersects the Demand line at that value. The farmer then draws a line from that intersection down to the x-axis, which is employment, and determines that, for example, four employees are needed. That seems to work."

"*Non, non*! To draw a metaphor from your computer industry, it is garbage in, garbage out. Keynes did not make a mathematical error. He made an input error. The guiding factor for Investment, new business investment, is not the profitability of hiring new employees, but the viability of the business concept after totaling all the costs, analyzing the competition, and considering initial investment costs, the ease of entry into that line of business, and numerous other factors.

"It is imperative that you see this difference, Peter. It is risk that determines the entrepreneur's willingness to invest. If a new enterprise has little risk or few obstacles to overcome, the entrepreneur will invest and the hiring of new employees will follow. The x-axis on the graph should not be the number of employees but the amount of business risk. Do you see the difference?"

"Are you saying an economy only grows when risk is low?"

"Peter, you are on the right track. Keynes thought it was the amount of money in consumers' pockets that determines whether an economy grows, but it is not. It is the confidence of entrepreneurs that investment in a new business has low risk. Where low risk prevails banks will create new money to loan for investment. The money does not need to be in anyone's pocket. 'Aggregate demand' is nonsense. There is no Mt. Everest encouraging entrepreneurs to invest, because it is there. A government making money available does nothing to spur economic growth if the risks are too high. No one will attempt a peak if the slopes are too steep."

"You have said a lot. Let me sort this out. Are you saying Keynes doesn't understand the operation of the banking system?"

"Oui, Monsieur, he fails to appreciate that banks can borrow and that fractional lending laws allow banks to lend up to ten times the amount they have on deposit. Since banks rarely lend up to their full capacity they are not restrained by deposits. Keynes' formula that savings equal total investment (GT p.-63) is incorrect, when fractional banking investment can equal ten times the savings on deposit, investment is not constrained by savings."

"What does this mean for Keynes' idea of inadequate demand causing the employment problems during the Great Depression?"

"It means he was wrong, very wrong. It means the solution was right at his doorstep, but he pushed the world in another direction. He had the chance to save the world economies when he simplified my ideas into 'Supply creates its own Demand (GT p.-25),' but belittled my message, instead of championing it. I showed that a new business creates the lending space to fund a new economy. His misunderstanding brought unnecessary tragedy to millions of households across the world. The man should be vilified not worshipped."

7 : Michelle

"Mr. Say! Mr. Say!" someone calls from across the pond. It is a young woman, running down the west causeway toward us. In our discussion about Keynes' famous model we absentmindedly walked out of the Scholar's Study and continued on the pathway around the garden to stand below the 'mountain'. The young women came around the boathouse, knees pumping beneath her pleated skirt. "I am so glad to find you. Excuse me." she says coming to a stop, bending forward, and then slowly straightening her back, catching her breath, placing her wrists on her waist with her hands folded to the rear like a sprinter reaching for a baton.

"You must be Henry's daughter," said Jean Baptiste.

"Yes, I'm Michelle Tang. Huh, so nice to meet you. Huh, huh, oh excuse me—I'm still out of breath. I feared I wouldn't catch up with you." Michelle extends her hand like she is meeting a head of state. Jean Baptiste obliges in an equally formal manner, taking her hand by the fingertips and gently lifting them in a gesture of a royal greeting a commoner.

I get a whiff of the sweet tropical fragrance she must have applied before meeting us. I say, "I'm Peter. I met your father at the restaurant." *I assume her father filled her in about the mysterious Mr. Say. I must find an opportunity to pull her aside and get her view on what is going on.*

"Nice to meet you. My father said I could join you on your walk. Is it okay? I'm an economics student at Portland State University. I would love to hang out with you for a while."

"*Mademoiselle*," says Jean Baptiste in a sweet endearing tone, "we would be delighted to have a fellow student of economics lead us through the city."

His tone seems a bit much. I wonder if Michelle finds it offensive.

But Michelle quickly adapts to her role. "Oh, I was hoping you would let me tag along. Let me stand here a moment to catch my breath."

I have never been in a discussion about Keynes with a bubbly economist. This should be interesting.

"Have you enjoyed the garden? It takes my breath away, like now."

"*Oui, oui, Mademoiselle*, it has been a delightful stimulant to the senses."

Oh, my God, deliver me from this torture!

"When I first saw you I thought you were missing the garden's attractions. You were both just walking with your heads down, looking at the path."

"Obviously, we needed to be interrupted," I interject.

"What do you mean by that?" Jean Baptiste says in an offended tone.

"I just meant that when a conversation gets so deep one loses touch with reality, it's time to stop. We had reached that point. Jean Baptiste had just made a brilliant point about the IS/LM model. Michelle, are you familiar with the IS/LM model?"

"Oh, yes. We studied that in school. I did my Senior Thesis on the IS/LM model."

I look at Jean Baptiste's furrowed brow. I haven't yet secured his forgiveness, and now Michelle has shocked him with her interest in Keynes. "Michelle, you make a valid point about needing to look up from the path. Let's walk to the top of the 'mountain' and look up, out, and forward!"

"I agree," says Jean Baptiste. "I would like to see more of the garden."

We turn around to start up the fifty-step mountain trail, but our path is blocked by the Black Widow and Snidely Whiplash, who apparently have come down from the viewpoint just above our head. *How long were they there? Did they overhear our conversation? Why are they following us?*

We stand aside and let them pass then start up the trail. Michelle remarks, "That was an ominous looking pair."

Thank you, Michelle, my thoughts exactly.

"It seems people prefer dark clothing in this city," Jean Baptiste says.

"People want to fit in on the ant pile," I say.

After an uncomfortable pause Jean Baptiste says, "Michelle, in addition to his expertise in insect behavior, Peter is a student of Asian art. He was telling me about the tools of the Chinese scholar inside the study shortly before you arrived."

Michelle glances in my direction, "Oh? Please continue."

I wait until we arrive at the top of the 'mountain' before responding to Michelle's request. The 'mountain' is a stack of rocks designed to look like a distant peak with a waterfall and stream emanating from a cave underneath the mass. Although the summit with a flat top for viewing is only twenty feet high, the location offers a stunning view of the entire garden.

"Michelle, see that building in the corner?" I point to the Scholar's Study. "Inside is a typical merchant's study with the four 'Friends of the Scholar' laid out on top of the desk. I explained to Jean Baptiste the use of the ink stone and the ink stick, and was about to give him a little insight into the brushes. If you're both interested, I'll continue."

"Oh, please do," says Michelle. "I'm curious about Asian arts, because I'm Asian but my family has not taught us much about our heritage."

"You know that brushes come in different sizes and shapes. In ancient times they were made from a variety of different animal hairs. The best brushes were a mix of hairs from more than one animal. Some of the prized combinations included at least some mountain goat, fine rabbit hair, and yellow weasel. The different hairs change the characteristics of the brush. Particular hairs allow the brush to pick up more ink, for instance, or to release the ink on the paper as smooth as glass or with ridges like the bark of a tree."

"So interesting, I would love to learn more."

"Here's a story you can pass on to your children when you get old and grizzled like me.

The first hair from a baby's head was often added to a scholar's favorite brush because it was thought to bring luck in the imperial examinations."

Jean Baptiste shuffles his feet and refocuses on the view. *I think my dissertation on brush construction bored him.*

"Is anyone else starving?" Jean Baptiste asks.

"Starving? You've got to be kidding me. You just ate a pizza a couple of hours ago!"

"Not starving, but I could use a pastry. Michelle, can I interest you in a pastry?"

"You can, and I know just the place."

Jean Baptiste offers her his arm and the two of them walk off hand in hand sharing giggles.

After about ten steps, Jean Baptiste turns and says, "Peter, are you going to join us?"

"Yes, as soon as I get my stunned off."

"*Mademoiselle*, do you know what he is talking about?" says Jean Baptiste closing the conversation door and escorting Michelle away.

Michelle answers politely in a slight whisper, "Peer is stunned that you're hungry again."

"Oh, I see. The English are a bit strange sometimes. They want to turn a simple remark into some clever observation."

"They are imaginative people."

8: Voodoo Donuts

I chase down my companions as they head for the exit. "Where are we going?" I ask.

"I want to take Mr. Say to Voodoo Donuts. Do you think he will enjoy that zany experience?" asks Michelle.

"I am sure he will—excellent idea. Let's see what he prefers, a croissant or a Voodoo donut? Do you know any of the history of Voodoo Donuts?" I ask, slipping in just behind the pair. "I read an article in *Willamette Week* a couple of years ago. Listen to this, Jean Baptiste, the owner is French, isn't he, Michelle?"

"I would prefer to listen to Michelle. Please continue your story, *Mademoiselle*."

I better watch my p's and q's or I am going to lose my place in line.

We leave the garden and walk toward Burnside Avenue. Jean Baptiste falls behind to smoke. He takes out a Calabash pipe from his left jacket pocket, a classic Sherlock Holmes variety with a coffee-colored stem with a white Meerschaum bowl on top of the gourd. The pipe goes into his mouth, and from his right pocket he pulls out a clump of tobacco stuck between his fingers. He carefully rolls the tobacco between his thumb and first finger, methodically sprinkling the crushed leaf into the bowl. He strikes a match on the brick wall of the building as we're walking by and lights his pipe.

Michelle picks up the story. "The owner is not French. He only has a French nickname, *Tres*. I imagine he is Irish since his real name is Richard Shannon the Third—a prince of fun from the emerald isle."

"Now the truth comes forth. He is Irish, maybe a nearby relative of yours Peter" notes Jean Baptiste. "Is he crazy? Does he have a red beard and unruly hair?"

"Guilty on all counts," answers Michelle.

"One of your band of brothers, Peter? One of your merry men?"

"I'm not going to run from the obvious."

"Now I am interested," says Jean Baptiste, chuckling under his breath. "Michelle, please continue the story of this legendary businessman."

"Tres was born here in Portland. Some consider him to be the city clown."

"A court jester, that fits," says Jean Baptiste.

Jean Baptiste, you're showing your true French colors.

Michelle continues, "In an article printed in the *Willamette Week,* they described his dress as 'Keebler Elf gone deadhead.' His black dog is named after an African-American television host, Oprah Winfrey. And at his house, the walls of his bathroom are covered in Ringling Brothers and Barnum & Bailey Circus clown pictures."

"Nothing unusual about this typical Irish businessman," says Jean Baptiste with a grin.

Michelle says, "On weekends Tres plays tambourine, gong, and cowbells in a performance called 'Karaoke from Hell' at Dante's, a bar across from the original Voodoo Donuts. Oh, and the bar has a sign written across the back exterior wall of the building that says 'Keep Portland Weird'."

Michelle has Jean's Baptiste's full attention, and I'm listening to be courteous.

"Tres has made a bundle from his popularity. Voodoo Donuts is one of the city's biggest tourist attractions," she tells us. "The shop mirrors Tres' zaniness. He sells his donuts in pink boxes with two dancing witchdoctors across the top. People who order three dozen donuts, get their purchase in a coffin shaped box. It's crazy, but it works."

"Oh, we must get a coffin of donuts. Don't you think, Jean Baptiste?" I suggest facetiously.

"Oui, Monsieur."

Michelle continues, "The store is sooper popular. Almost any time of day or night, there is a line out the door and halfway to Burnside."

As we stand on the north side of Burnside waiting for the traffic light to release us to the world of the living, I say, "We're almost at the day-glow temple of donut indulgence." I point out the neon sign on the corner with a line of people queued up as if at a movie theater, with stanchions connected by rope in a serpentine pattern to keep the crowd in check. "That's Voodoo Donuts."

We cross the street and Michelle and Jean Baptiste surge ahead to get in line. I follow, drawn more by obligation than by any taste sensation. I look at the crowd we're joining. A large group of dancers in purple tights stands just outside the door. There is a family group dressed in matching sweats in the shade of green that is the 'official color' of Oregon. In front of them is a couple escaped from Gold's Gym, clothed in their prison garb. The largest inmate proudly displays his gang colors, purple, green and red, in a tattoo extravaganza that covers his forearms. I catch up to my companions, who are surveying the crowd about their favorite donuts.

"What flavor is the Voodoo Doll donut?"

"They're each a little different, but the classic is the chocolate Voodoo with raspberry jelly filling and a pretzel stick through its heart. But before you bite it, be sure to give your donut a name," says a twelve-year old girl, holding the crowd's attention.

"Name your donut after your enemy! Then press the pretzel stick in a little deeper and chomp down on the head—yum," explains a petite eight-year old donut expert interrupting her big sister.

"One of my favorites," says a muscular brute in a skintight tank top at least two sizes too small, "is the bacon maple bar with crispy bacon on top—a complete breakfast without the cholesterol and fat of a fried egg."

The gym rat's girlfriend is next to offer a suggestion: "Have a Portland Creme, the official City of Portland donut. It's *delish*. It's a chocolate donut filled with Bavarian cream, and it has two eyeballs on top representing the 'vision of the city'. The eyeballs are very close together......The city is cross-eyed."

The excitement over the menu doesn't end. A young member of the Purple Prancers judging by his attire, suggests, "You should get the Cock'n'Balls."

"Jeffrey! Shush." Jeffrey rises up and turns away from us as the father chaperoning the dancers takes control of the young trouble-maker.

Jean Baptiste asks me privately, "Is the donut anatomically correct?"

I whisper, "As you might expect, it's covered in chocolate frosting and filled with a triple serving of Bavarian cream."

"*Oh, mon Dieu!* It is no contest. Voodoo wins! One point for Voodoo donuts!"

The line moves quickly, and Michelle brings us back to reality. "Get ready to order. Any questions?"

"Let's do a triple witching," I say. "Everybody get a Voodoo Doll, and we'll stick it to Keynes. I am going to get a coffin so we have a selection."

We take our donuts outside where the sun is breaking through the overcast to make it quite pleasant. The adjacent alley has been closed to vehicle traffic and picnic tables installed for customers of the nearby eating establishments. We walk halfway down the alley and choose a table. "Let's eat." We open our coffin and peer inside, each of us devising an eating strategy.

I direct the others. "Before you bite off the head of your Voodoo doll, name it 'John Maynard Keynes', explain why he deserves to be decapitated, twist the pretzel stick, and then go for it."

"John Maynard Keynes, you deserve to..." we all say in unison and then fill our mouths with his bloody raspberry essence.

"Jean Baptiste, is this a pleasurable experience?"

"Ah, le meilleur! Sucré. Sucré. Sucré."

"Sweet. Sweet. Sweet," I mimic.

"Why are you two so down on Keynes?" asks Michelle.

"Oh, *Cerise*, we need to explain. Peter, I will let you do the honors. My little brown Keynes is sticking to the roof of my mouth," says the ever-dignified Mr. Say.

"Jean Baptiste, you need to savor your victory—eat slower. Michelle, the issue is around Say's Law. Do you recall from class that Say's Law was described by Keynes as 'supply creates its own demand'?"

"Of course."

"My gluttonous friend here takes exception to the way Keynes described his view of supply."

"Ov curse, excurse me," JB mumbles through a mouthful of donut.

Michelle and I look at Jean Baptiste, who shakes his head like something has a grip on his throat. He chews largely, moving his jaw from side to side, and swallows. "Ur, I take exception because he turned my theory about supply inside-out with his short pithy phrase. I was explaining how to rescue an economy stuck in the mud. Keynes used sarcasm to shut me up. He humiliated me. For a hundred years the world has endured unnecessary financial downturns, because Keynes belittled me."

9 : Economic Slumps

"You see, Michelle, before Keynes all economists agreed that supply creates economic growth. It does not guarantee it, but supply puts in place the dynamics or potential for economic growth. I use the term potential because a product might not have a market or a market large enough to sustain the producer."

JB continued, "One example is a flying car like the Moller sky-car, which was envisioned first in the 1960s, but so far the vehicle has failed to achieve free flight without reliance on ground effects. The concept has appeal, but the vehicle does not have enough lift to fly or to do so economically. This invention is an example of a supply idea that will not create its own demand. Even though huge sums of money have been spent on engineering and building prototypes, it has not been enough yet to overcome the engineering obstacles and create a market."

"That was a strange example. There are examples of new products that do," says Jean Baptiste.

"Yes there are, but first let me clarify for Michelle that Keynes turned Jean Baptiste's basic concept into an absurdity. Before we talk about business successes that prove Jean Baptiste is right, let's look at how Keynes used his definition of Say's Law to attack my gentle friend here," I say, wrapping my arm around Say's shoulder.

"Keynes argued that if Say's Law is true, then every business idea generates capital that circulates, encourages investment, and in the extreme case produces unlimited employment. Keynes pointed out that if that were true, the Great Depression would not have happened, since business couldn't suffer a slump. Keynes said the solution was not supply, but a lack of demand. If people had money in their pockets companies would sell products and maintain their labor force."

"Just like I was taught in school," Michelle chirps.

"Ah, Michelle, but Keynes skipped over the Moller sky-car effect: lack of market interest, not lack of demand. People want a car that flies, but not when performance is sub-par. In the Great Depression people were unsure of the future so they stopped investing, stopped buying beyond the necessities, and this changed the dynamism in the economy."

"Michelle," I continued, "remember that when Jean Baptiste wrote his theory, the economy was not explained through supply and demand models. That explanation was developed sixty years later by Keynes' teacher, Alfred Marshall. Jean Baptiste's explanation was not in terms of supply and demand, but in terms of market health. He followed Cantillon' idea that upsetting the market causes slumps because it changes the risk balance of the community or state. In the Great Depression passing the Smoot-Hawley Tariff Act led to punitive retaliation that decreased international trade in a couple of years by 50%. Which is an example of a government action that went terribly wrong. Another is the Federal Reserve's action to keep interest rates high in order to comply with Congress' mandated currency to gold ratio. Cantillon in his time observed slumps and dips in employment and ascribed the cause to government interference in the market. Jean Baptiste, didn't you caution that regulation can be useful and proper, but not to prescribe the nature of the products and the methods of fabrication?"

"Yes, this is what I wrote: 'It is not by nature, but ignorance and bad government that limit the productive powers of industry (TOPE loc. 1470-71)."

"Essentially, bad government policy causes slumps."

"*Oui*, Professor."

Michelle opens the donut box. She says, "I can't afford any more calories, but I want to taste a few more of these. Do you mind if I cut off some small pieces?"

"*Mademoiselle*, be our guest."

I continued, "Let me summarize, it's government that causes slumps by passing laws that impede normal economic activity. In our recent slump, government interference in the home lending market prequalified people who didn't have the resources to be homebuyers. The result was the second largest economic slump of all time. The biggest slump, the Great Depression, was caused by the Federal Reserve Bank's failure to reduce interest rates in a slowing economy and Congress' imposition of tariffs that upset international trade."

"So you two believe Keynes was wrong when he used his supply and demand theory to justify government deficit spending during the Great Depression, and that these same ideas caused the Great Recession," Michelle clarified, licking chocolate off her fingers with a birdlike flicking tongue.

"That's part of it. Jean Baptiste feels an obligation to set the economics world back on its axis, and he wants me to help."

"Are you going to do that? Please do, and help my generation get the economy moving," requests Michelle.

"It's a difficult problem. I'm not sure if I can do it."

"We began our walk to give Peter time to think about it," Jean Baptiste adds.

To avoid making a commitment, I start another topic. "Michelle, before you arrived, Jean Baptiste told me that Keynes' definition of the terms in the IS/LM model reflected his lack of knowledge of fundamental business processes. He simplified business investments to a simple addition of input costs minus selling price to calculate the profit. It is not that simple. The potential market must be evaluated, the ability of competitors must be assessed and investment funds must be secured."

"*Mademoiselle,* do you see how that his mathematical view is not a market perspective?" Michelle stares at Jean Baptiste without speaking. "Let me explain," Jean Baptist says. "As businesspeople we seek opportunities to sell more products. Market conditions are paramount. We ask ourselves a number of questions. Is there an unserved market? Is there a market niche I can exploit? Is the competition in the market segment weak? Is there a product people cannot find in their market? Introducing a new product or service begins with an analysis of the profitability in the market. Keynes made a fundamental error in assuming business begins with an analysis of how much a company can earn off its employees. Business does not operate that way."

"My dad was right, you guys are pretty sharp."

"That's a good lesson for you, Michelle. Your dad is probably right about many things."

"I understand that! But Peter, are you going to help Mr. Say?"

"I'm considering it since Jean Baptiste shared his convincing evidence of flaws in Keynes' thinking. But before I go home and lock myself in my office to write, I need equally strong arguments supporting Say's position in the modern world. I also may need more ammunition against Keynes. He has a huge army of followers. I am not going to do it if there is any doubt of success."

Pushing the last bite of his Voodoo Doll into his mouth, Jean Baptiste asked, "If that is what we need to do, let us begin by proving that my so-called Say's Law is correct. Keynes' restatement of my theory, that 'supply creates its own demand', is false. I never said that. The closest thing I said is that 'a product is no sooner created than it, from that instant, affords a market for other products to the full extent of its own value.' (TOPE: Loc. 2563-66).

"Had I known this passage would foment controversy, I would have stated it better, but it is a very simple idea. Listen closely. From the moment a product is sold the seller has money in his pocket to spend on other products or services. A manufacturer might buy raw materials to make another product. A little girl might take her lemonade money and buy some candy. A land developer might take his money and buy another piece of land. In all cases, the money returns to the market to purchase another product. This is the way an economy grows. Each new product expands the market. There is no other way to expand an economy. Lowering interest rates does nothing without a product in the mix. Hiring a 1000 new employees does nothing unless they produce a product. Not only is my idea the method to expand the economy, but it is the only way to do so."

Jean Baptiste looked down at our donut box and points at a glazed donut half covered in purple sprinkles. "What is that?"

I answer, "That's a Grapeade."

"Grape flavored? I will try that one. *Mademoiselle*, will you join me?"

"I am over my limit."

"I'll join you in sweet gluttony," I say, and reach for a Dirty Old Man, a cake donut dipped in chocolate with pieces of Oreo cookie on top, covered with a peanut butter drizzle.

I lean back on the bench, close my eyes, and let the sun bathe my face in vitamin D. When I open my eyes again I see the Black Widow and Snidely Whiplash sit down only a couple of tables away.

Michelle leans across the picnic table and says, "We have visitors."

"I noticed. It must be time to move on."

Completing his consumption of the Grapeade donut with his rapid chipmunk chomps, Jean Baptiste says, "Before we do anything else, I want to stop by my hotel."

"Sure," I say. "Where are you staying?"

"At the Benson. Do you know where it is?"

"It's only a couple of blocks from here. We can walk."

"Good, I need a smoke after eating."

Fearing a breach of social etiquette, I remind Jean Baptiste, "Remember the rules. No smoking in restaurants. That applies even when sitting outside at a restaurant table. So wait until we leave and start our trek."

"*Oui, Monsieur,* I will comply with all state and local regulations. I am so happy the government defined where I am allowed to smoke and not to smoke."

Michelle asks, "Do most Frenchmen smoke?"

"*Non, Mademoiselle,* only the cultured."

"Mr. Say, why is Keynes held in such high esteem?"

Michelle please hold-off on those questions until we move out of earshot of the women and man in black. "Let's get into that as we walk to the hotel."

As both my companions gathered their belongings the conversation continued, but they didn't move away from the table. "*Cerise,* it is a matter of timing and of the institutions he supported. Mathematics in economics was a new trend. Keynes was first and foremost a mathematician. He used the novelty of the technique to 'prove' his economic concepts. Keynes was also a loyal government employee. His allegiance to his employer was complete and his employer was effusive in his appreciation of Keynes' loyalty."

"Oh, so mathematical trickery and the old boy's club came into play," Michelle says.

"True, *Mademoiselle*, but mathematical formulas have a long history of tripping up clear thinking in economics. In my *Treatise*, I described the effect of mathematics on economic writers this way: 'The mathematical cast given to their reasoning by these writers, has captivated and led astray the understandings of intelligent and sagacious readers, induced them to adopt, as scientific truths, what, when properly investigated and analyzed, are found to be merely specious hypotheses.'" (TOPE loc. 313-15)

"Wow, that is a direct attack on mathematical proofs of economic theory," says Michelle.

I see the significance of this thought and want to probe further into this, "How could Keynes advocate deficit spending when his supply and demand type model is about the money supply and employment? Doesn't an increasing money supply indicate people and companies are reducing their investments? Also, doesn't increased government borrowing compete against private borrowing? As a taxpayer aren't I obligated to repay all government debt? It seems like that would make people anxious and unlikely to spend."

"Good inquiry, Peter. You are asking the right questions. 'Capital alone is not sufficient to put industry in motion.'" (TOPE loc. 7541)

"It seems to me," says Michelle, "that Keynes used a supply and demand type chart for two quantities, employment and money supply, to show when people and companies will invest, but the reason for investing and hiring more employees is unclear to me."

"You are right on the money," I say.

"Michelle," says Jean Baptiste, "your natural perceptions are impressive. You are correct. Investment and employment are the goals, but does government borrowing encourage investment? No. Does government borrowing encourage hiring? No. Keynes' model might imply that it does, but in the world outside of his models it does not work."

I interject, "Jean Baptiste, are you saying that the point where the supply and demand line cross is only a result of mathematical inputs and does not reflect the real world?"

"Correct. Keynes' mathematical formulation is not the way business operates. Businesspeople start at the other end of the equation. They look at how many products are desired and at what price. They do not begin by adding up all their costs at various employment levels and intersect that line with their desired profit to determine the size of the factory. Entrepreneurs begin the other way. They determine the size of the market and calculate if they can deliver the desired products at a price the consumer is willing to pay and still make a profit."

Michelle says, "I see, entrepreneurs don't decide to open a business based on a calculation of the number of employees that generates the highest profit. That's ridiculous. Sorry, Keynes. It also makes sense that the number of products that the market wants would be the starting point for an entrepreneur. I never realized Keynes had such flawed logic underlying his General Theory."

I notice over Jean Baptiste's shoulder that the black widow couple seems to be hanging on our every word. It makes no sense that this handsome couple should be interested in our technical account of economics.

"Good work, you two," I say. "Let's head up to Jean Baptiste's hotel."

Jean Baptiste takes out his pipe and Michelle picks up our trash. "What should I do with our half full coffin?" she asks.

"Would you like it?"

"Not for me, but the boys in the dorm would love it."

"Don't tell them who donated it," I suggest.

"They won't care."

I look up to see Jean Baptiste halfway up the block. He stops, lights his pipe, and takes a quick drag. The pipe droops in his mouth as he drops his hands to straighten his shirtsleeves. He pulls his right cuff toward his wrist and exhales the white smoke between his pursed lips then immediately draws the smoke into his nose, like steam expelled from a pressure valve. The hurricane force of his inhalation pulls all the smoke into the two sides of his septum like two steam locomotives racing side-by-side into twin tunnels.

"We better catch up with our leader," I say to Michelle.

10: Central Role in Economy

The three of us walk away from Voodoo Donuts, heading west toward downtown. "It just registered with me. How does a Frenchmen, dead for 200 years, pay for a hotel room?" I ask Jean.

Smiling and prepping his pipe, Jean Baptiste answers, "With a credit card."

"How did you get a credit card?"

"It came in the mail."

"Unbelievable. Have you used it?"

"*Oui*, last night in the hotel lobby I had a glass of Burgundy. Can I interest you in one when we get there?"

"Thanks for the offer, but I don't drink. I don't get the boost of confidence it gives most people. I just get dizzy and feel lousy in the morning. It's something I choose not to put myself through."

"And you, *Mademoiselle*?"

"I'm only twenty."

"Twenty, what does that mean?" asks Jean Baptiste

"Legally, she can't drink for one more year," I say.

"Why?"

"It's against the law to drink until you're twenty-one," says Michelle.

"*Sacre bleu*, what kind of government is this? I have never heard of such an outrage. Outlawing a drink, what possible reason is behind such an idea?"

"It's intended to reduce traffic deaths caused by drunk driving," Michelle says in a small wispy voice.

"What? The government is protecting people from their own lack of self-control? What will government think of next to justify its existence?"

After more of a stroll than a walk, we arrive in front of the magnificent facade of the Benson Hotel. The Benson is a landmark building designed by famous turn-of-the century Portland architect A. E. Doyle. The French Second Empire-style building has 287 rooms—it's a favorite stop for U.S. Presidents visiting Portlandia.

"Eighteen presidents, from William Howard Taft to Barrack Obama, have stayed in this hotel. JB, are you staying in the Presidential Suite?"

"No, I chose a more modest room. Do you want to come up? I am going to take off my coat and put on something lighter for the weather."

"No, I'll wait for you in the lobby," I reply.

"I'll wait with Peter," says Michelle.

We walk up a couple of steps and enter the magnificent lobby. The high, coffered ceiling is held aloft by huge pillars wrapped in now-extinct, dark Cicassian walnut imported from Russia. Elegant Austrian crystal chandeliers with silk shades hang throughout the space. Michelle and I sit down on an embroidered divan in the bar area. Jean Baptiste proceeds up the south grand staircase to his room. He stops on the landing halfway up to assess his appearance in a fourteen-foot high mirror made to reflect the entire lobby from that perspective. He runs his fingers through his hair, reassesses his appearance and then, satisfied, continues to the rooms above.

I look at Michelle, wondering what she thinks of Jean Baptiste's obvious vanity, but she is gazing elsewhere about the space.

I gesture toward one end of a walk-in fireplace bordered by an immense grandfather clock with nine brass chimes. My timing is impeccable as just then the mechanism fills the lobby with melodic tones. Michelle smiles at me.

In front of the fireplace are four Edwardian chairs arranged for conversation. The sophisticated space is further defined by an oriental carpet, and animal print stools arranged directly in front of the crackling fire for lucky children to use. At the corners of the seating area, Oriental black lacquer cabinets sitting regally on gold leaf finished bases complete the ensemble. A perfect resting spot for the regal and academic.

Michelle is looking at the room with her mouth open, entranced by the magnificent setting. Peter changes her focus, "Ironic, isn't it, that Jean Baptiste would choose a hotel environment that perfectly fits his nemesis."

"What...what?"

"Are you impressed?"

"Oh yes, I've never been here before. What were you saying?"

"Just that this hotel, with its history of eighteen presidential visits is more in the fashion of Sir John Maynard Keynes than that of our rolled-up sleeves cotton industrialist."

"Hmm...I see...you picture Mr. Say checking into a Marriott more than here."

"Or maybe even a freeway motel."

"Be kind, Peter. He has the stature to belong here."

"Do you like him?"

"Oh yes. Thank you for letting me tag along. Since we have a moment, can you fill me on the conversation I missed before I found you?"

"Be glad to. There's not much to tell. We made note of Keynes' view that the government should manage the economy and Jean Baptiste's view that the economy is best controlled by market forces."

"Am I right to say that Keynes was the first economist to suggest that government regulate the economy through control of interest rates and the money supply?"

"I'm not sure if he was the first in that respect, but certainly he was the first to suggest that government was better equipped than the market to control the money supply and adjust interest rates. That's the heart of the difference between Keynes and Say. Keynes argued persuasively that government had the intelligence and wisdom to properly direct the economy, better than the 'animal spirits' that roam the market. Ironically, Keynes never lacked in 'animal spirits': he performed quite successfully among the bulls and bears in the stock market.

"I'll tell you one of my favorite stories about Keynes' boldness. As a young man, shortly after being hired by the Treasury, he attended a speech by Lloyd George, then Chancellor of the Exchequer, about the economic position of France. When Lloyd George finished he asked for questions, Keynes replied, 'With utmost respect, I must, if asked for my opinion, tell you that I regard your account as rubbish.' Keynes never shirked from offering his opinion."

Michelle twists her lips and turns her head to the side, deep in thought. "The man had guts. That is certainly needed at times, but it sounds like he may have chosen the wrong moment to be so assertive."

I respond, "He is given credit for an enormous brain, but he was not a theoretical economist like Say. At home in London, he was a mathematician and a stock speculator. He did not foresee the stock crash of 1929. Before October 1929, Keynes believed an event like the crash was impossible with the Federal Reserve overseeing the economy. See any irony in that belief?"

"You would think such a reversal might change his opinion of the wisdom of government management. How important an economist was Keynes in 1929?" Michelle asks.

"With Irving Fisher of the United States, he occupied the pinnacle of economic thought. Both men failed to predict the Great Depression and neither at the time could explain the event. It is the Great Depression and the devastating unemployment that followed that prompted Keynes to search for an explanation. The result of that inquiry was his primary work, *The General Theory of Employment, Interest and Money.*"

Michelle says, "Isn't it in that book that Keynes took exception to Say's view of the value of production? Please clarify for me the difference between the two."

"*The General Theory* is given credit for establishing a central economic role for government in western economies. The biggest difference between the two men's views is that Keynes characterized deficit financing, and public expenditures and consumption, as primary economic drivers. Say argued that the primary economic drivers are low taxes, private investment, and entrepreneurial initiative. It was at this moment a line was drawn between public and private. Keynes argued that government expenditures were more wisely directed than market expenditures."

"So Keynes felt we could borrow and spend our way to wealth, and Say argued we should shut-up and work," Michelle says with a smirk on her lips.

"Mademoiselle, it is more complicated than that, but that is the starting point. Keynes argued government intervention is essential during a financial crisis. Jean agrees government management of fiscal and monetary policy is important, but not to put government in control, only to incentivize the private sector. He saw government like the Moon or the Royal family—nice to have, but not essential."

"Oh, I love the Royal family. Can't you make cuts somewhere else?"

"History shows that most parliaments agree with you. I should point out that Keynes' theory was that 'aggregate demand' determined the level of economic activity. Keynes argued that more state spending of any sort (GT p.-129), including with borrowed funds would move an economy forward and upward."

"I know Keynes lived a hundred years after Say, but did Say foresee this argument?"

"Well, in a way he did. By arguing that supply was the factor to increase, and characterizing all government consumption as negative to the economy, Say was making the case that decreased government spending encourages consumer spending. Say also considered government hiring as a wealth destroying activity. He felt employment could only increase through an increase in private sector production."

"Who wins the argument?"

"Well, I may be biased, but I think Jean Baptiste has the stronger arguments. Keynes argued that employment in either sector puts money into the economy, but I tend to agree with Jean Baptiste that increasing employment in the private sector builds a business whereas a public sector investment does not produce a profit stream. The idea that public investments are equivalent to private investments that produce profits just doesn't pass the sniff test. Even Keynes cannot explain how government borrowing contributes to the economy. Profitable investments distinguish private from public investments. This difference is what distinguishes an investment from a purchase.

"Jean Baptiste makes a strong case that government interference causes economic slumps. Jean Baptiste also makes a strong argument that no one is going to go fishing in a hurricane regardless of the demand for fish."

"Keynes doesn't distinguish between the effectiveness of stimulating demand in all sorts of different economic conditions, does he?" observed Michelle.

"I think that's where Keynes loses the argument. He ignores the concerns of the businessperson and the consumer. He expects a robotic response even in the most adverse of economic conditions. For instant, lowering interest rates is not going to encourage someone to expand a business when the market is eroding. Keynes also expects consumers to buy when prices drop. Under normal conditions I agree with Keynes, but during a financial crisis, consumers change their responses."

"Earlier you asked me if I knew about the IS/LM model. How did that discussion conclude with Mr. Say?"

"Jean Baptiste explained most of that to you when he discussed how business development is complex and involves numerous factors besides labor costs and interest rates."

"Has he convinced you to write the book?"

"Possibly?"

"Doesn't showing the IS/LM model is inaccurate upset the Keynesian apple cart?"

"I believe it does, but we need a new cart to carry the produce to market. That's where I'm not confident that Say has a complete theory to replace Keynesian economics."

"You mentioned replacing the N factor, the number of employees likely to be hired, in the IS/LM equation with a risk factor to determine employment growth. I like that."

"Yes, but I don't have that completely worked out."

Michelle turns toward me like a crouching tiger ready to strike. "Can't you work that out in the process of writing the book?"

"Maybe, maybe not?"

"It sounds like you need to take some risk."

What's going on here? Have I fallen victim to a team of pushy economic zealots? What's the deal?

"Michelle, do you think this man is the real Jean Baptiste Say? Or am I making a deal with the devil?"

"The devil? Really, Peter!"

"I have concerns."

"You're an author. Does it matter if he is real or a figment of your imagination? You have a great story. A great story makes a great book. Don't write it for Jean Baptiste. Do it for yourself."

"I suppose you're right. You sound much too logical for an economist," I reply, protecting my fifty year-old insecurities from attack by a college economics major. "Michelle, are you part of a conspiracy to convince me to write a book about Say?"

"You've uncloaked me. I am Nina from Olde Towne Pizza, your intermediary to the spirit world. Ooooooooooh."

"You think you've fooled me, but I suspected you were a ghost. You don't eat enough to be a human," I say, trying to shake off my embarrassment.

Jean Baptiste walks up from behind and sits down next to Michelle. "*Salut*. I hope I did not take too long."

"Not at all. Michelle was just asking about our discussions before she met us at Lan Su Garden. I filled her in on the gory details."

Jean Baptiste adjusts his seat and looks around the lobby. "Guess who I just passed at the top of the stairs. The couple dressed in all black that sat across from us in Olde Towne Pizza and followed us to the garden."

"Oooooh, mysterious," says Michelle.

"Michelle just revealed her true identity to me. She is Nina, the ghost from Olde Towne Pizza. That makes her at least a hundred years old."

"Ah, *Mademoiselle*, you are a great beauty at your age. In your youth you must have been breathtaking. Do not make my old French heart ponder such wonders."

He sure can lay it on.

"Thank you, Jean, you raise my blood pressure."

Jean Baptiste wraps his arm around Michelle. "Peter, did you buy this young angel a refreshing beverage while she waited?"

"No, I was waiting to invite you both for a taste sensation just around the corner."

"*Mystérieux. Mademoiselle,* shall we partake of this adventure?"

"I'm intrigued. Let's go."

We walk out of the lobby. Jean Baptiste stops on the top step of the entry stairway to light his pipe. The bellman takes note and approaches; Jean Baptiste notices and quickly walks down the stairs to join us. When we reach the corner, I look back to see the bellman still waving his arms to cleanse the air of Jean Baptiste's pungent French tobacco.

We walk three blocks west of the Benson to a small chocolate shop I want them to experience. We come upon an ornate bronze Benson bubbler and I remark, "See this water fountain? Simon

Benson, whose hotel we just left, installed these fountains throughout the city." My companions bend over and taste Portland's clean, cool water.

11: Economics in Math Terms

"There is nothing better than cool spring water to sharpen the senses," spouts the French gourmand.

"The only thing more refreshing than clear crisp water is clever, compelling conversation with friends concluded with a sweet dessert," I insert.

We walk another block and I introduce them to the sweetest store in Portland. "Welcome to Cacao," I say, making a broad sweep of my arm.

"Du chocolate?"

"Yes, this store sells only chocolate products, from all over the world: Columbia, Dominican Republic, Grenada, Vietnam, Mexico, and Oregon, of course. Have you ever been anywhere so sweet?"

Cacao looks like a high-end coffee shop with its dark wood tables, bar, and back counter with stainless steel equipment. "This is quite the hot spot. I didn't know this place existed," admits Michelle.

Jean Baptiste walks over to a counter along the north wall and bends at the waist to peruse the selection. "I see no products from European manufacturers. Why is that?"

I explain, "The owners seek out products from small, specialty manufacturers that you are unlikely to find elsewhere. This is a chocolate tasting experience. Come up here to the tasting bar. I promised you a drink. Well, I want you to try their drinking chocolate." I turn to the bartender. "Can you pour us three *demitasses* of your Premium Drinking Chocolate?"

"Certainly." The bartender reaches under the counter and retrieves three cups. He says, "This chocolate is made with 74% organic Dominican and 68% wild Bolivian dark. It has a bold, slightly bitter flavor mellowed with intense sweetness. I hope you enjoy it." He places a small cup and saucer in front of each of us. Then he picks up each cup and turns to the back counter to fill each with hot chocolate from an espresso-like machine.

"What does the 74 and 68 percent mean?" asks Jean Baptiste.

"That's the percentage of cocoa in the chocolate; the higher the percentage, the darker the chocolate, the more bitter, and the more healthful."

"How is it healthful?" asks Michelle.

"Research has shown that dark chocolate stimulates the transformation of flavonoids in the cocoa that help improve arterial health. Some studies showed a 20% improvement in circulation."

Michelle, smiling and cuddling her hot chocolate, asks, "How many of these should I drink a day?"

"It's not a daily thing. Try once a week followed by a day of fasting," I answer.

Michelle leans in front of Jean Baptiste to get the bartender's attention. "What's your opinion about the health benefits of dark chocolate?"

"It takes only a small piece each day to get the benefits."

"How much is a small piece?"

"Most dark chocolate candy bars are divided into squares. Some scientists suggest eating a single square a day. A couple of bars should last a month."

"Only if you have immense self-control," I note.

Michelle says, "I think I will get a couple of months' supply. Jean, how many bars for you?"

"I am only going to buy a single bar. My blood is very thin. Peter, you're going to join us, aren't you?"

"With pleasure, but make your selections quickly—I want to walk through Powell's Books."

Surprised, Jean Baptiste says, "Oh, we are going to a bookstore, wonderful. Are you familiar with the English bookstore Shakespeare and Company in Paris? It is the most famous English bookstore in Paris."

Michelle blurts, "Jean Baptiste, I visited that shop when I was in Paris. With such a big reputation, I imagined a much larger place. I had a great time. It is so, so cozy."

Jean Baptiste says, "It has a small footprint, but many floors. It is not the size but the quality that matters. The shop attracted the likes of Hemingway, Joyce, and Stein. I enjoy going there for the traditions they maintain and the comforting aesthetic of old typewriters, the skinny aisles between stacks of books, and the cushioned benches for reading. They still provide lodging for artists and students, known as 'tumbleweeds', to work on their craft, in exchange for work in the shop."

"You'll enjoy Powell's Books," says Michelle. "They maintain some of those traditions held dear by the readers in this city. But it's not cozy until the rains start in the fall."

"It's also the largest new and used bookstore in the world," I add.

"I want to see that place. Here Peter, is my money and the chocolate bar I want to purchase. Can you do that for me while I step outside and have a smoke?"

"Sure. We'll meet you outside."

"Michelle, it occurs to me that we should go to Powell's travel section and review the recommended 'not-to-miss-spots' in Portland. I'd hate to overlook something."

"Perfect, let's do that."

After Michelle and I pay our bills, we meet up with Jean Baptiste and walk the three blocks to Powell's Books. We enter at Eleventh and Couch, walking past the famous book column that supports the canopy over the entry. We head past the information desk to the elevator bank and the Weird Book Wall.

"This is the Weird Book Wall," I explain. "It's an eclectic selection of books that either have the word weird in the title or present an unusual perspective by the author."

"Peter, should we look for your book here?" Jean Baptiste says, stifling a belly laugh.

"I would be delighted to have it displayed in such a prominent location, but I am afraid it is shelved with the dusty old economics books on the next floor up."

"Next to the works of prominent French thinkers, no doubt—quite a distinguished location," notes my modest French friend.

"Well, let's go upstairs and see," I suggest. "The economics books are in the Rose Room just above us."

We walk up the stairs into the Orange Room and turn right to enter the Rose Room. After passing a half dozen aisles, we find the economics books. Jean Baptiste begins following the author's names, back and forth from the top shelf and slowly down to the floor.

With drooping eyes expressing his feelings Jean Baptiste notes, "They have none of my books."

"They don't have my book either," I say.

Michelle sweeps in like a tidal wave to refloat our drowning spirits. "They're probably just sold out."

It's a nice thought, but the only time one of our books would be on the shelf is if the used book buyer made a mistake.

I say, "Jean Baptiste, don't be disappointed. You're a historical figure, so let's look in the indexes of the popular economics textbooks and learn what is being taught today about you in school. That should be interesting."

"*Oui*, I will settle for that."

"Michelle, pick out some of the prominent textbooks. We can go up to the Coffee Shop and look through them."

We gather four thick economics textbooks, two by Paul Samuelson—a 1964 edition and a 2001 edition, a 2008 textbook by Roger Le Roy Miller, and the principle economic text used at Harvard, written by the Dean of the Harvard's Economics School, N. Gregory Mankiw.

We proceed back to the stairs and descend half a floor to the mezzanine level and then through the Gold Room into the World Cup Coffee & Tea room. We find a table and lay out our books. I give Miller's text to Jean Baptiste because I think it will have the least incendiary interpretation of his theories. Michelle takes the Mankiw text because that's the one she uses in school. I spread out the Samuelson texts in front of me—his works were the bible when I went to school.

I tell them, "This is going to be fun. Let's start with the definition of Say's Law in each book and Jean Baptiste can tell us which is the most accurate.

Jean Baptiste shakes his head. "Oh, my, Mr. Miller allocates two pages in a thousand-page textbook to summarize three hundred years of economic thought. Then he uses Say's Law only to set up a study of Keynesian economics. He is a Keynesian."

I say, "It will be hard to find any modern economist who's not a Keynesian—that's what they all were taught in school. How does Miller define Say's Law?"

He reads: "'Say's Law is defined as 'Supply creates its own demand; hence it follows that desired expenditures will equal actual expenditures.'"

I ask, "Is that a correct definition?"

Jean Baptiste looks deflated, "First, I never summarized my theory into such a pithy phrase. Second, my theory is not about 'desired' and 'actual' expenditures. My theory is an explanation of how making a new product increases the wealth in an economy. My theory is about the benefits of production. The act of production puts money into the economy through the entrepreneur's spending for raw materials, labor, etc. Since this expense must be recovered by the entrepreneur to repay his bank, and in doing so his actions cause the total wealth supply to increase."

I try to paraphrase. "The key is that this is new money the entrepreneur asks the bank to create for him. This new money adds to the old money already being used in the economy. You're saying that each product thrown into the economic pool creates new monetary ripples as other entrepreneurs borrow to create products to absorb this new money. There is nothing about desires or mathematical equalities in your theory. You're just saying a product dropped into the economic pool will create new money ripples, right?"

"That is correct. Every new product adds to the supply of money. The new money creates the potential for a bank to fund another business idea."

"So instead of some absolute quality, each product creation is potentially the impetus for new business," I suggest.

"Peter, I like that, it is a valid way to think about it. Product creation produces new money and new money provides the potential for growth, it is fertilizer you sprinkle on the economy and growth is guaranteed. The entrepreneur's promise to repay gives banks the power to support an entrepreneur's dream, but the entrepreneur needs to act on his dream or nothing occurs. Most economists think, and Keynes thought, that if you add 'x' to the economy, 'y' will happen. The reality is that if you add 'x,' 'y' is possible. It takes a bank and an entrepreneur to release the potential of the new 'x'."

Michelle looking squarely at Jean Baptiste's eyes as she spoke, asks, "How does the banking role fit in with Keynes' theory?"

"Keynesian economics is all about equilibrium, the point where supply and demand cross. I am about increasing supply and pulling demand upward. Maybe not always at the same pace, but fast enough to increase production, profits, wealth and employment. There is no best level—only a push to do more. Creative ideas by entrepreneurs and supportive lending banks makes that possible.

Jean Baptiste looks down at Miller's book, then looks up again and says, "I see that Miller, like Keynes, justifies his theory with mathematics. In my book, I wrote: 'Some writers maintain arithmetic to be the only sure guide in political economy; for my part, I see so many detestable systems built upon arithmetical statements, that I am rather inclined to regard that science as the instrument of national calamity.'" (TOPE, loc. 3552)

12: Width of Economic Growth

"Let's look at how the distinguished Harvard economist, N. Gregory Mankiw, depicts Say's Law."

Michelle looks up from Mankiw's textbook. "I can't find a reference to Say's Law or to Jean Baptiste Say. There's no listing in either the index or the glossary of economic terms. That is strange, because I remember the phrase, 'supply creates its own demand. I must have heard it in a lecture."

"Jean Baptiste, so sorry, but our most distinguished university chooses not to present your theories to their student body. I apologize."

"Peter, this explains why your nation's economic management is so backwards and shallow. The so-called modern progressive philosophy promoted in your collegiate system is neither progressive nor modern. It is the top down control system first perfected by the Chinese and the Egyptians more than four thousand years ago.

Your economic system follows parameters proven wrong at least five hundred years ago. I find it deflating that your most prominent university will not even give the market system a fair hearing. Outrageous! How can you support such a travesty?"

"I cannot."

"I would hope not," replies Jean Baptiste, smoldering with anger.

"Jean Baptiste, I've made my decision. I will help you explain how the market system operates."

Michelle gives me a big hug. "Oh, Peter, that is wonderful."

Jean Baptiste shakes my hand. "Pete, I am proud to have you as a partner in this crusade."

"And I'm proud to be a member of your team, but I'm also aware of how difficult a task we are accepting."

"What worries you the most?" asks Michelle.

"The desire of economists to understand everything in terms of supply and demand charts will make my task difficult. We must overcome the Keynesian theory of aggregate demand or we will not make headway in the academic citadels."

"Do you have an idea how that can be accomplished?" she inquires.

"I feel the key is Keynes' failure to evaluate the confidence of consumers, businesspeople and investors as prominently as interest rates and the size of the money supply. He understands the importance of confidence in these three groups, but since the level of confidence is difficult to quantify Keynes uses interest rates and money supply as surrogates, but I wouldn't accept this challenge, if I thought it was impossible. There is hope."

Jean Baptiste smiles. "Do not forget to focus on Keynes' bias toward government management versus management by the market. In the Keynesian approach, from a long line of unemployed workers, a few individuals leave the line to go work on repaving a road, but return to the line a year later. In the market approach, a new company introduces a new product. The company and its suppliers add a few employees here and there and eventually across the globe, expanding the entire economy while the employees retain their jobs long-term. This is the difference between a wax-plug solution and a permanent fix."

Michelle thoughtfully asks, "Can you explain the business sector view in a standard supply and demand chart?"

"No, you can't since a permanent job is one job and a wax-plug position is one job. The charts are identical."

"Good," Michelle effuses, "I love the idea of not using supply and demand charts to represent employment."

Jean Baptiste says, "But without a strong visual representation how do you undermine the notion of aggregate demand. I think you are right, Pete, that concept needs to be slapped down."

"Jean Baptiste, you amaze me. Darling, where did you hear that expression?" asks Michelle.

"I heard it on the street when I was lagging behind you two, having my smoke. Which reminds me, how about another walk so I can take a drag or two? Michelle, are you finished with your coffee?"

"I am finished and ready to go."

I take a last sip of coffee and rise to my feet. "Where should we go?"

"How about the Chinese elephant in the Park Blocks? It will make a nice connection with our visit to Lan Su Garden? We missed it earlier when we stopped at the Benson?"

"*Mademoiselle*, your idea is delightful."

"The Shang Dynasty Elephant it is," I agree.

We gather up our dirty dishes, put them in a plastic tub to be washed, and head for the street.

"This is the world's largest new and used bookstore, and they do not carry a single volume of my book. I am stupefied."

Michelle and I look at Jean Baptiste. Neither of us can find appropriate words to say.

"You two go ahead. I will light up and commiserate by myself."

We start down the hill as directed, not speaking a word.

The Shang Dynasty Elephant is a life-size bronze replica of the much smaller Chinese original. When Jean Baptiste arrives he is struck by the majesty of the sculpture: "*Magnifico.* It reminds me how ageless a great work of art can be. Even today, five thousand years after its creation, there is still a market for this piece of art. Can you imagine if a government committee had designed this elephant?"

"It would be the size of a watermelon, to save on shipping costs," I observe.

Michelle: "It would be made of papier-mâché so it could be recycled."

Me: "It would have none of the religious symbols inscribed on its back, to avoid offending other religions."

Michelle: "It would be a combination of both African and Indian elephants."

Jean Baptiste: "It would be made in America."

Michelle: "It would have a Planter's Peanut decal on its shoulder."

Me: "There would be a plaque acknowledging the Democrat politicians who helped acquire the sculpture."

We all have a good laugh. I say, "Michelle, where to next?"

"Since everyone is in such a good mood, how about the Faux Museum? It's just a couple of blocks from here."

"*Mademoiselle*, with the overwhelming success of this stop I will follow your lead." Jean Baptiste fills his bowl with tobacco once more, and we continue our walk down Burnside.

"Let's talk about aggregate demand," I suggest. "First, let's clarify aggregate demand is just total demand. Demand is the amount of products or services consumers want to buy. Keynes used the term in constructing his supply and demand charts as he tried to find the cause of high unemployment. It is not a term like interest rates or expenditures based on what happens in the market, but a summary of demand used in his explanation of high unemployment."

"Why is that important?" asks Michelle.

"I just want to make sure we recognize that this sum is the total of products and services consumers buy in a given period."

"Duly noted," says Jean Baptiste, following behind me with a trail of smoke following him.

I continue, "Aggregate demand is sometimes defined as the final value of all goods and services that individuals, firms, government, and foreign traders buy at various price levels. Another definition is the total of all planned expenditures in an economy during a year. It is something close to GDP but without accounting for inventories and salaries for certain government employees.

Suddenly, we hear shouting behind us where JB is walking. "Put out your smoke old man. This isn't your ash tray. This a public park. Kids play here. My wife and I want to inhale clean air, not your putrid stinky exhaust. Stop polluting the environment."

Jean Baptiste immediately responds, "So sorry, I thought I could smoke here. I will put my cigar out." He drops his cigar and begins to grind it into the ground.

"What the hell. Do you think this park is a landfill? And what is it with your accent, are you some foreigner? Do you think we Americans, built and paid for this park so you could come along and throw your garbage into it?"

"No, no, I am so sorry."

"YOU'RE PART OF A GROUP of foreign gay invaders intent on converting our athletic male heterosexuals into your cult of sexual perverts. Aren't you? Promoting cock waging parties to satisfy your pervert fantasies. THAT'S IT ISN'T! ISN'T IT."

"HEY, LEAVE THE GENTLEMAN ALONE," said Henry Tang from the intersection on his way home. "Now get out of here. And I mean, now. That's better."

Just catching up with Jean Baptiste, I recognized the Chef from Old Towne Pizza and saw the attackers make a quick exit. I thanked Henry Tang from lunch, "Thanks for intervening, he's an obvious target, but totally harmless. We will stay closer to him. Can we buy you a drink? Your daughter is a delight."

"Thank you, but I am heading home. Get your old friend a drink. He probably needs it more than I do. Thanks anyway. Hey, sweet," he said waving to his daughter and turning to continue his trek uphill.

"Merci Beaucoup," squeaked Jean.

"That was an unsettling moment, let's sit down on those benches over there" I said pointing to a group of park benches. After five minutes of silence I said, "Let's not let the terrorists distract us from our mission of solving the economic problems of the world. Let's see, we were concluding that Keynes definition of Aggregate Demand and GDP were close enough for amateurs."

"*Oui*, that provides an overall sense of what Keynes meant by aggregate demand," Jean Baptiste acknowledges.

"Simplifying Keynes' thought," I say, "when people buy less, the economy slows. Your idea, Jean Baptiste, is that when companies produce less the economy slows. Agreed?"

"*Oui.*"

"Keynes' idea was, when the economy slows, you need to have the national government spend more, and to incentivize business investment by lowering interest rates. Correct?"

"*Oui.*"

"Your idea, Jean Baptiste, is to encourage companies to produce more by removing impediments to production such as trade barriers and high tariffs. The opposite of what was done in the Great Depression. Or raise residential lending standards in a time like the Great Recession to strengthen the quality of real estate bonds. Again, the opposite of what was done at the time.

"Creating favorable conditions for entrepreneurs and investors to succeed reinforces the economy. Their success will encourage more business. More business means more jobs and more jobs means higher wages and fewer defaults. Do I have that right?"

"*Oui.*"

"Jean Baptiste, you don't really see a need for special government policies in an economic slump?"

"*Oui*, if government policy is properly focused, then slumps will not occur or they will be mild. In any case, the solution is not some radical new idea, but simply more of what moves the economy. Any action at all should simply be an exercise in fine tuning."

"Keynes said that the economic crisis was caused by a change in the amount of money available to purchase products. With less money people changed their buying and investing behaviors. That is more than fine tuning," I comment.

"I agree that is more than fine tuning, but the cause of the wallet shrinkage was not the sudden disappearance of money, but the Smoot-Hawley Tariff and a drought on the Great Plains," Jean Baptiste elaborates.

"The solution was not the creation of the Works Progress Administration and crop subsidies. The solution was to repeal the Tariff and relocate the farmers to areas with adequate moisture to grow wheat," I add.

"Peter, I see your point. Keynes' focus on demand as the source of economic vitality is not supported by the historical record. I particularly like your point that total spending varies in its significance to an economy. An economy might spend an immense amount, but because of taxes or other inefficiencies produce little profit. In such a situation, the economy will slowly stagnate, because there is insufficient capital to support new entrepreneurs. Total spending is not the single or most important criterion for a vibrant economy."

"Then what does propel the economy and keep it healthy, wealthy, and wise?" Michelle asks.

Jean Baptiste puts out his pipe and says, "Mademoiselle, it could be the number of new opportunities in a society? There is some evidence that an economy with numerous niches open to growth fares better than an older, more competitive economy."

I ponder this for a moment. "Are you telling me a vibrant economy suckles on market flexibility or receptiveness?"

"A very French way to express it." Jean Baptiste compresses his lips and moves his head slowly up and down. "Market receptiveness might be the right term. It captures the idea that growth depends on political openness, consumer willingness to be adventuresome, and consumer resources sufficient to support new approaches. Peter, I think you should make that view part of the explanation why aggregate demand is not a good explanation of a healthy economy. 'Market receptiveness' captures more of the nuance and depth of the commercial marketplace. I like it. How about you, *Mademoiselle*?"

"It makes sense to me. Just adding money to the economy is wasteful, temporary, and undirected. An approach that captures the interest and some of a consumer's money is likely to last and form the foundation of new industries. I should also point out that we have arrived at the Faux Museum. Do you want to go in?"

"*Oui, Mademoiselle,* I am a big fan of museums. Is that the right word?"

"Well done, *Monsieur*. Fan is perfect."

"Michelle," says Jean Baptiste, "I will take care of the tickets. You lead the tour."

Michelle holds back the curtain that hides the 'museum' and signals with her hand for Jean Baptiste to enter. "Slip behind the curtain, and experience the wonders of the Faux Museum. The exhibits are loosely based on how a high school carnival would be set up in the gymnasium. It is intended to be *kitschy*. Do you know what *kitschy* means?"

"Is it something close to silly?"

"Very similar, but the best *kitsch* has an adult sensibility. I don't think that's been achieved here. Let me explain the exhibits. A common game at the carnival is the bean bag toss where you try to throw a beanbag through the open mouth of a roaring lion."

Michelle reaches down and picks up a beanbag, holds it for Jean Baptiste to touch. "Look over here," she says, pointing to a large cut-out animal. "They've taken a woolly mammoth body, added an oversized ant's head, and cut a large hole in the side. This is called the 'Woolly Ant Bean Bag Toss'—fun, fun, fun, at least, for the creator."

Michelle throws the beanbag into the hole in the side of the woolly mammoth-ant. Jean Baptiste stands motionless, his mind apparently baffled and unable to find a satisfactory resting spot.

Michelle continues, "The next exhibit is the Road Kill Petting Zoo. I guess that's self-explanatory. Let's move along to 'our' most popular exhibit, the Turd Toss. Here, Jean Baptiste, took a rubber turd and flung it into the outhouse. Points are scored if your turd goes into the outhouse hole." Michelle holds the turd out for her guest. Jean Baptiste does not take the turd. Michelle throws the turd into the small structure and misses the hole, scoring no points for anyone.

"Oh look," she squeals, "over here is an exhibit by the Science Fair winner, Bryon Wayne Huff, on how to make crack cocaine." In a more explanatory tone she says, "To enjoy the humor here requires a particular perspective."

"The perspective of a ten year old boy?" says Jean Baptiste.

"It's a Portland thing, but I hope it gives you some appreciation for how informally we take ourselves."

"*Mademoiselle,* do not be embarrassed. We Parisians invented *avant-gardes*. Most art misses the mark, but the effort is always interesting. It was good for a giggle or two. Where is Peter?"

"I think he abandoned us to save the $5 ticket fee."

"I am not surprised, the cheapskate, but that is what makes him a good economist."

Jean Baptiste opened the exit door and noticed me standing on the sidewalk. "Oh, Pete, there you are. I am going to have a long smoke after this. I need to go to La La Land, as you Americans call it, and ponder what I just experienced," he says with a big grin. He turns back toward the museum and braces his back against a nonexistent wind to light his pipe.

Michelle looks worn out from her role as tour guide. "Thank you," I tell her. "That must have been drudgery."

"Oh, it went fast, but the parody did not translate. Let's stay in the real world."

"I agree. The real world is difficult enough to describe. Shall we head back into the city to see more of the iconic sights of Portlandia, including the namesake statue of the city? Jean Baptiste, we have a copper beauty similar to the Statue of Liberty that your fine country gave us as a gift. This one is called Portlandia and she kneels above the entry to City Hall."

"Sounds delightful; a tourist stop I would like to visit," replies Jean Baptiste, leaving the Faux Museum in his dust.

"It's a bit of a hike, so you'll have plenty of time for a good smoke. We may make a few intermediate stops."

"Fine. You and *Mademoiselle* lead the way."

Jean Baptiste follows us only with his eyes until we are half a block ahead: a courteous gesture appreciated by his two non-smoking companions.

13: Money Supply

Michelle and I walk down the sidewalk in the direction of City Hall.

"Why do you think Jean Baptiste is so driven to correct Keynes?" Michelle asks.

"I don't know *who* he is, much less *why* he is on this mission."

"Maybe, he is Mormon."

"Clever, smart ass."

"He is an enigma, but does it matter who he is?"

"It sounds like you're in the same place I am. I recently had a similar experience in Seattle with his partner in mystery, who claimed to be Richard Cantillon. I finally concluded it didn't matter who *he* was. The ideas matter, but the person is really only a carrier."

"I'm sure Jean Baptiste appreciates that more than you or I. That could be why he is so driven."

"Since he is French I suspect it has something to do with their concept of *la gloire*."

"I'm not familiar with the expression."

"There is no good English equivalent. In fact, in Anglo-American culture we are told not to do things for glory, but many of the greatest French achievements were done for *la gloire*. I think the distinction is that in our culture glory is an individual trait, but in French culture it is a group trait. It involves a sacrifice that an individual makes for the good of his country."

"That makes sense to me. Jean Baptiste deflects your questions about his personal goals because he wants to correct Keynes for the glory of the French."

"I get a sense of that as well. He sees the French as a big family, a family under attack. I think he also feels that the Englishman Keynes did not respect the legacy of French economic theory. He is trying to restore French analysis to its rightful place. I suspect that the grating arrogance of John Maynard Keynes is particularly painful."

"Keynes is known for his elitist persona."

"Michelle, you are right about that." I hold out my coiled fist for a pump.

Michelle gives me a short quick tap with her tiny fist. She says, "Don't you think it is ironic that Keynes is now put on a pedestal by the party of the working class when he believed in the ruling class' superiority."

"Irony almost seems too mild a term. He was a product of his upbringing. At Cambridge he joined an ultra-secretive intellectual society, the Apostles. The Apostles viewed themselves as superior people."

"Peter, am I right that the Apostles were contemptuous of middle-class values and morality?"

"Yes, they rejected such middle class values as thrift, savings, and building for the future. Most of those values did not apply to the wealthy of Cambridge. This caused trouble when they used their high social positions to enter government service. In the employ of the government, they never felt constrained by a need to be financially prudent or plan for the future. We are now suffering the consequences."

"Do you really think the world's excessive use of debt is directly related to Keynes?"

"I hate to be so simplistic, but yes. Before Keynes, economics was a set of methods people used to make their lives better. It was business: how to sell more products, how to make more money, how to be more efficient, how to attract more buyers. The solutions were businesslike: take your apples to town, wash and polish your apples, pack your apples in straw so they don't bruise, build a covered stall along the road.

"Keynes came along and said, 'Let government loan you some money at low interest so you can purchase more land and hire more workers. Pay the government back and in the end you will be richer. If you don't believe it, I have a chart here that proves this is the best path for you to follow.'"

"It sounds persuasive to me."

"Keynes' plan is persuasive, but it is not correct. People are seduced by the sermon, but never evaluate what is actually being said because it comes from the 'holy' government. It is an age-old fraud."

"That sermon makes me question what Say is saying, not Keynes. It's not easy to disagree with our leaders, especially tall attractive ones."

"Precisely. That's why what Say is asking of me is so difficult."

"Just a moment ago you were willing and confident."

"Oh, I still am, but I don't want to minimize the difficulty of the task."

"This all makes me uncomfortable."

"Don't be. Say has a famous quote that explains the problem: 'With no fixed opinions in relation to the causes of public prosperity, the nation, like a ship without chart or compass, was driven about by the caprice of the winds and the folly of the pilot, alike ignorant of the place of her departure or destination.' This is Keynes' Achilles' heel. Keynes doesn't understand the purpose of economics.

"Peter, surely you don't think you can sell that idea to a skeptical public."

"It may be difficult, but no one said it would be easy. I just have to convince people that Economics is a method to make life better. Economics is a group of tools that when applied makes life sweeter. Some early economists thought it was a system to ensure fair distribution of production, but it's not. It's a system to help each person get more of what they want. Keynes tried to make economics a model, but it is not a drawing of an orchard or even a set of instructions. It is a shovel, plow, reins, horse, and water buckets. Economics is a set of tools to protect or increase the productivity of each individual. It has nothing to do with the right of the state to oversee economic policy or tax the land. Those are political decisions, not economic. Economics has everything to do with helping the individual provide for his family. In such a system, the wealth and power of the state are not the goals or even a consideration. It is an important consideration for people who get their wealth and power from the state, as Keynes did. I can appreciate his conflict of interest."

"That is much better. You had me worried. I was afraid you didn't have a strong challenge to Keynes' view," Michelle says in a reassuring voice.

"Keynes' appeal is his belief in an elite class. He argued for top down control by this class, as has every dictator and oligarch from the beginning of time. Say, on the other hand, believes there is no elite class and that everyone should have a role in the economy. He argues that people should get to cast votes for their personal economic interests in the market."

"Okay, I get all that, but most people believe Keynes, because they want a job. He said that government should create jobs in times of financial stress. That is very appealing. How are you going to counter that argument?"

"Employment depends on business expansion and you cannot expand business by waving your hand. My approach is to show that Keynes' model is flawed, and then review history to highlight the conditions when business growth was vigorous."

Michelle stares at me, her forehead wrinkled. "Your case against the model is key. Most economists do not challenge the model. They attack his promotion of deficit spending as proof of skewed thinking. That's not enough."

"I agree. Here's my argument against his model. We can describe people in words or depict them in paint, but I know of no number that describes the complexity and intricacy of a person. Are you a 7, or a 10, or a 70,856? It is meaningless. Any theory based on assigning numbers to human actions is flawed. I have an extremely hard time getting beyond that idea to seriously consider Keynes' mathematical models. His models seem like a kindergarten picture of a person with a circle head, two black dots for eyes, a short curved line for a mouth, a vertical line for the body, and four angled lines for arms and legs. How does that illustration help me understand what decisions a person will make or when they will lose a job? It's so ridiculous that I cannot find an adequate way to criticize the approach. It is fine for a child, but for an adult it's just lazy scholarship. Keynes should be ignored and economic study should begin from the point a new product is produced, like Jean Baptiste proposes."

"Good picture," Michelle smiles.

"Most critics of Keynes fail to challenge the mathematics. I will show that employment is not a function of demand, $E \neq f(D)$. "

Michelle twists her mouth in anticipation of more. "That's a good start, but what *is* employment a function of? Employment must have a relation to some financial factor."

"Obviously. As Say states, it is a function of supply: $E = f(S)$. If you create more products, you need more people to make them."

Michelle gives me a smirk. What does that mean.

"Supply, in turn," I say, "is a function of Risk: $S = f(R)$."

"Brilliant," says Michelle, raising her arms in a V above her head. "It is so simple. What keeps people from hiring? Fear. Remove the risk and there is no fear. I love it. I know you can write this book."

"Stem your enthusiasm. I want to make sure I am right. I must propose the idea to Jean Baptiste."

"Sure, but in the meantime let me propose that you name your theory the Risk Cross."

"Clever. You have naming authority. I'm sure Jean Baptiste will agree. Let's wait for our leader and then show him the world's smallest park."

"Is it far?"

"No, it is only twenty feet away."

"No way! There's nothing around us but a four lane street and a bunch of buildings."

"We are on Naito Parkway, named for the Japanese businessman who, starting in the 1970s, revitalized the rundown district of Old Town, where we met. He coined the name 'Old Town', and led the restoration of more than twenty buildings in the area. As you might expect, he was an economist.

"I am a big fan of Bill Naito. He represents the best of the Portlandia attitude. As an example although he was Japanese, not Chinese, he was one of the leaders that arranged for the installation of Lan Su Garden. Even the neon sign of the leaping white stag that greets visitors crossing the Burnside Bridge is a Bill Naito recovery project. His biggest contribution, however, was not his buildings but his civic leadership on urban transportation projects such as light rail, the trolleys, the streetcar system, and this pedestrian friendly roadway into the city."

Jean Baptiste joined us. He knocked the ashes from his pipe into the street gutter and put the pipe away in his frayed coat pocket. "You two had an active walk. I noticed you chattering away the entire length of this road."

"I was telling Michelle about some of the people I know who lived here in the 1980s."

"Why are we stopping here?" he asks.

"We are here to enjoy what is the world's smallest park, according to the *Guinness Book of Records*."

Jean Baptiste, adjusting the scarf around his neck, looks up the street and turns a full 360 degrees. "I see nothing."

Michelle says, "Is it that concrete circle in the middle of the street, with the cute little tree?"

"*Correcto mundo!*" I exclaim. "That two-foot diameter circle is Mill Ends Park. In the 1940s a journalist named Dick Fagan, a good Irishman, watched out his office window as the city drilled holes in this busy street for new light poles. For some reason, the workers chose to move a pole slightly and drilled a new hole a few feet away. They never came back to fill the first hole. Dick Fagan wrote a number of articles in his column, which was called *Mill Ends*, about the hole. One day he saw a leprechaun digging in the hole and rushed out from his office and captured the little sprite. This trick forced the leprechaun to grant him a wish. Dick asked for his very own park. Since he did not specify the size of the park, the mischievous Irish spirit gave him the light pole hole as his park. Eventually, Fagan filled the hole with soil and planted some flowers. Fagan described the dedication of the park in 1948 as the site of the 'only leprechaun colony west of Ireland.' Patrick O'Toole, the resident leprechaun, made many appearances in Dick Fagan's column and often can be seen around the park on St. Patrick's Day."

Seeing my audience's rapt attention and open mouths, I continue, "After Fagan's death in 1969 the park lived on in various forms. It was once a swimming pool for butterflies, complete with a diving board."

"The 'Keep Portland Weird' motto fits this place," says Jean Baptiste, reaching around his neck to fuss some more with his scarf. "Can we stop for a bite somewhere?"

I turn and look at Michelle. She just shrugs.

"We're not that far from the Heathman. How about we go look at the Portlandia sculpture at City Hall and continue up the hill to the Heathman Hotel for dinner in their restaurant?"

"I like that plan," says Jean Baptiste.

Moving in next to Michelle, Jean Baptiste asks, "*Mademoiselle*, what is this famous sculpture Peter is leading me past?"

Michelle fluffs her hair out from behind her coat collar. She says, "It is a copper *repousse'* sculpture of a goddess welcoming visitors to Portland, similar to the Statue of Liberty in New York harbor."

Jean Baptiste says, "Did you know your Statue of Liberty was a gift from the people of France to the people of the United States? It was constructed in France and shipped to the United States in pieces for reassembly."

"I knew that. Did you know the American people built and paid for the base with donations?"

"The average donation was less than a dollar and many of the donations came from schoolchildren," I respond.

"Did you know our funding for the Statue of Liberty also came from schoolchildren and the common people throughout France," replies Jean Baptiste.

"Did you know besides the work of the French sculptor Bartholdi, the head and arm were formed with assistance from Viollet-le-Duc, the restorer and engineer of Carcassonne?"

Jean Baptiste parries, "Did you know that Gustave Eiffel replaced the statue's original masonry super-structure with a steel curtain wall system? A similar system would be used fifty years later to construct the high-rise office towers of New York City."

I reply, "Did you know the American poet Emma Lazarus was asked to donate a poem to help with funding? After initial resistance, she penned a poem with the lines, 'Give me your tired, your poor, your huddled masses yearning to breathe free'–the words now inscribed on the base of the pedestal."

Jean Baptiste smiled at Michelle. "That sentiment captures the feeling both countries shared about the power of liberty. Did you know a breath of freedom invigorates a country?"

I add my bit to the conversation. "I couldn't agree more. Did you know that the Statue of Liberty was primarily a private project? Both the U.S. Congress and the New York state legislature tried but were unable to pass funding legislation. Then it was newspapers that spearheaded private funding initiatives."

Michelle grabs Jean Baptiste's arm. "Look halfway down the block. There she is, bending down to welcome visitors to City Hall." Michelle points his arm toward the sculpture.

Jean Baptiste holds his mouth open in a gasp for three seconds then says, "*Magnifico, Mademoiselle.*"

As we walk toward the sculpture I say, "The image comes from the Seal of Portland, and was executed by Pittsburgh sculptor Raymond Kaskey in 1985. The sculpture is about 35 feet tall, but if the goddess stood up she would be half the size of the Statue of Liberty."

"Standing directly below, it makes quite an impression," says Jean Baptiste. "There is striking commonality between this piece and the Statue of Liberty in the welcoming gesture. Both pieces say, 'Come forth, join us, throw off your chains.'"

"Do you think that relates to economics?" asks Michelle.

"*Mademoiselle*, I am struck by the particular message they convey. If the Liberty were leaning on a shovel instead of holding a torch, an economic message would be conveyed. Likewise, if Portlandia were located above the entrance to Intel, a different message would be sent. Government is a recognized symbol of social freedom and liberty, but not of economic opportunity and security. Freedom and liberty are something we all expect, but economic opportunity and security are equally as precious."

14: Profit

"Why can't government ensure both? Freedom and economic opportunity." I ask.

As Jean Baptiste reached into his pocket for his pipe he seemed to sense that our hike was beginning again, "Government and the business sector are opposites. Government is about rules, about molding society, about conformity and beliefs. Business is about rule breaking, mold breaking, individualism and new ideas. It is an oil and water proposition. Can I have a smoke while we walk to the Heathman?"

"Sure. We'll walk up the hill and past the elk sculpture over there," I say, pointing to a traffic circle with a bull Thompson Elk gazing warily to the north.

"You two proceed, I will follow. Do either of you know anything about this elk?"

"I don't. Michelle?"

She says, "It was donated to the city by a wealthy 19th century businessman."

Jean Baptiste says, "Perhaps it has no civic purpose beyond a glorification of nature's magnificence. Most civic sculptures honor politicians, military heroes, or a principle of governing such as liberty, equality, or freedom. This sculpture does none of that."

"Should the city have a monument to business?" I ask.

"It would be nice if civic leadership recognized the contributions of the marketplace to society. Without the creativity of the entrepreneur none of these expensive sculptures would be here," Jean Baptiste noted through the pipe in his lips as he pulls down first his right then his left sleeve. Properly straightened-up, he expels smoke from his lungs and quickly sucks it back in through his nose.

Michelle wrinkles her upper lip and grabs my sleeve. "Let's go."

Propelled by her tug, I follow her quickly into the intersection and up the hill past the elk, to separate us from Jean Baptiste by nearly half a block "I think we are safely out of the pollution," I say.

"I can't stand his smoking."

"You have made that quite obvious."

"His coat must be fifty years old and he smells like the inside of a cigarette butt."

"It's part of his French mystique," I say in defense of my new friend.

"There's no mystique: he just stinks. I'm going to let you have dinner with him by yourself. I need to get back to my dorm and my schoolwork. I shouldn't have taken half a day."

"I hate to see you leave. It was a delight to have you accompany us." I look back and see Jean Baptiste at the bottom of the block, walking slowly and adjusting the scarf around his neck. "We're planning on having breakfast tomorrow morning at Mother's Bistro & Bar at 8 a.m. Can you join us?"

"Let me think about it. My first class is at 11. If I can make it, I'll text you. What's your number?"

"Here's my phone, call your phone. I'll explain to Jean Baptiste, and we can meet, hopefully, tomorrow morning at Mother's."

"Thanks, Peter," Michelle says, waving goodbye to Jean Baptiste. He seems to think she's signaling him to speed up. He takes two quick steps but then settles back into his slow slog.

The light changes and Michelle crosses the street, headed south on Broadway toward PSU. I look back down Madison and wait for Jean Baptiste.

When he finally makes it up the hill, I ask, "Are you ready for dinner?"

"I am ready to sit down and rest. Where is Michelle?"

"She left to go back to the college to study. We may see her again tomorrow at breakfast."

Jean Baptiste is too tired to ask for further clarification. I point across the street. "There's the Heathman. Just one short block, and on the flat."

Jean Baptiste absentmindedly empties his pipe bowl by banging it against the bumper panel of a two-door gullwing Mercedes-Benz SLS AMG. The car alarm barks, "MOVE BACK, MOVE BACK!" followed by a recording of gunfire.

Jean Baptiste stands petrified. Fortunately, the light changes on Broadway. I take his arm and lead him to the center of the street. "It's all right, you merely set off the car theft alarm."

"MOVE BACK, MOVE BACK!" the alarm shouts. Then comes the last movement of Tchaikovsky's *1812 Overture* with church chimes clanging and cannons firing.

"Keep walking, we're almost there." We reach the Heathman entry and I literally push Jean Baptiste into the lobby.

"Did I do that?"

"I am afraid so. The owner will come out and shut off the alarm shortly. Let's go to the men's room and wash up while the commotion subsides."

In the dining room, the hostess seats us at a table overlooking the street. We look outside but the Mercedes is gone and its spot is already occupied by a Prius. "I guess you're safe," I say.

"What did I do to make the car upset?"

"Every Mercedes is touchy. Any bump and they scream hysterically."

"Is that what I did? Bump the car."

"Good fun! Yes, when you knocked your pipe against the side of the car you set off the alarm. All that ruckus was a recording intended to scare you away. The car's computer is programmed to play the recorded sounds when it senses a bump."

"All of that commotion started from disposing of the smoldering ash in my pipe bowl. It is a good thing I did not spit the phlegm from my mouth–I might have set-off explosions."

"You're right! If the owner had seen you, you might have been shot."

"You must be kidding!"

"Exaggerating, but not by much. People here are sometimes violently protective of their expensive possessions. I'm sure that car is worth more than $100,000."

"Are the police looking for me?"

"Probably not. You only left a smudge and some ash residue on the side of the car. But I would recommend you not do that again."

"I will not. I have learned my lesson. I was extremely frightened. I almost left Portland."

"Don't do that. We need to talk more about this book you want me to write. I can't do it alone."

"I am not sure I can help you anymore. My head is spinning and filled with the sound of gunfire."

"Jean Baptiste, all you need to do is rest and the memories will fade. Change your focus: open your menu and let's find some delicious food to settle your stomach."

"Can we start with some wine?"

"Absolutely. Here," I say, handing him the extensive wine list, "find something that appeals to your palate. Let's order appetizers to accompany the wine. Does either the Potted Duck Confit Rillette or the Country Rabbit Paté sound appealing?"

"The confit would be my choice. The rabbit sounds too gamey."

"I agree. Let's get something civilized like force-fed duck."

Jean Baptiste turns to the French wine listings and runs his finger slowly down each page. "I suggest a Vouvray for some light tart sweetness to accompany the *paté*. Either a Domaine de Vodanis Sec 2001 Vouvray from a Huet vineyard, or a Foreau Vouvray Sec."

"Either is fine. You choose."

"If you leave it to my judgment, I select the Domaine de Vodanis."

"Do you like braised beef short ribs? They have an egg dish here with spinach and *Mornay* sauce that accompanies the ribs that is to die for."

"That sounds wonderful. Please order it for me."

A waitress approaches and says, "Good evening. Can I be of any assistance to you?"

Jean Baptiste takes his head out of the wine menu, straightens his posture, composes his countenance, scans the waitress' face and curls the corners of his mouth into a smile. "*Mademoiselle,* you can be most helpful. We want to order some appetizers."

Our waitress is dressed in a white shirt and black skirt—she has short straight black hair combed down from the crown of her head to just above her ears. Her look is quite French. Perhaps she reminds Jean Baptiste of his homeland. "Have you gentlemen decided what you would like?"

Jean Baptiste nods and points to the menu. "We would like this *paté* and a bottle of the Domaine de Vodanis."

"The Vouvray is a fine choice to accompany the *paté,*" our waitress says, sending a smile toward Jean Baptiste. "I noticed you two conversing intently—would you also like to order your *entrée* at this time so you can eat without interruption?"

"Please, that would be wonderful," I say.

Jean Baptiste says, "You will still visit us?" He gestures in my direction. "I could not tolerate spending an entire meal with only this boring fellow. Will you stop by to break the monotony?"

She briefly looks at me to check my reaction and, seeing that I am not upset, answers, "*Monsieur,* I will set aside extra time to check on your wellbeing. Now what can I get you for dinner?"

I say, "My French friend here would like the *Oeuf Mollet* & Rib Florentine, and I will have the *Bouillabaisse*."

"Excellent. Those are two of our most popular dishes and are prepared with fresh and local products. I am sure you will enjoy them." She bends down to place Jean Baptiste's napkin on his lap. "*Monsieur*, if anything is not correct, please speak to me and I will have it corrected." She walks around to place my napkin, but I have already pulled it apart and placed it on my lap.

"Gentlemen, is there anything else I can do for you?"

"We're fine," I say. "Thanks for the courteous service."

Jean Baptiste looks around the restaurant and then, apparently realizing I am still sitting across from him, says, "I was thinking about our book and how Keynes states that the circulation of money leads to a multiplication of the money supply. Am I stating that correctly?"

"As I recall, in your *Treatise* you deride the idea 'that a sum of money, by passing through twenty different hands, is equivalent to twenty times its own value. (TOPE loc 597)' Are you asking me if Keynes held this belief?"

Jean Baptiste smiles, "My disguise failed. I was just thinking this would be an easy Keynesian tenet to disprove, and easy to show how government spending does little to boost the economy."

"That is one of Keynes' vulnerabilities. He believed in something that today we call the 'fiscal multiplier'. The idea is that an increase in consumption spending will stimulate producers to spend more than the dollars spent by government. This is Keynes' primary argument for government deficit spending. He argued that one dollar of consumption spending equaled one-plus dollar of business spending. (GT p.- 115) The Great Recession is a very visible reminder that Keynes' theory is wrong. The more than two trillion dollars of stimulus spending and deficit borrowing did nothing to increase business spending or pull the economy out of the recession."

"Can you use those facts to illustrate the falsehoods in his theory?"

"When I talk about the circulation of money, I could expose Keynes' failure to discuss or even understand the importance of profit."

"It explains why his theory is so far afield. In my *Treatise*, I explained that 'in whatever class of industry a person is engaged, he subsists upon the profit derived' (TOPE loc. 1309-11) from his work. Profit is the cornerstone of the economy. Without profit, nothing would be produced."

"I take it you give no credit to Keynes' idea that increased government spending will stimulate an economy," I inquire.

"Peter, do not joke with me. The only spending that expands the economy is in the business niches that have a potential to generate a profit and produce returns sufficient for employee security."

"Would you conclude that increasing the circulation of money is the wrong approach to reviving a slumping economy because it does not create lasting employment or businesses?"

"Can a juggler increase the number of balls in the air by throwing them up faster?"

"For a moment."

"Then they all come crashing down."

Jean Baptiste is on a roll!

I say, "Do you think Keynes was wrong about the ability of stimulus spending by government to revive a slumping economy?"

"'The saints and Madonna of superstitious nations, the splendid pageantry and richly decorated idols of Asiatic worship, gave life to no agricultural or manufacturing enterprise.'" (TOPE loc. 2275-76)

"I'm confused by your response. Are you saying that any action that doesn't create new businesses, or expand existing businesses, will fail?"

Jean Baptiste responds with his classic line, "'[A] product is no sooner created, than it, from that instant, affords a market for other products to the full extent of its own value. When a producer has put the finishing hand to his product, he is most anxious to sell it immediately, lest its value should diminish in his hands. Nor is he less anxious to dispose of the money he may get for it; for the value of money is perishable.'" (TOPE loc. 2563-66)

I furrowed my brow, trying to put this puzzle together. "You are saying that a onetime injection of money by government won't work to kick start the economy. Why? Is the only way to create economic momentum to allow manufacturers to produce? Any attempt outside this process is futile?"

"*Oui*, business cannot be forced back to life with a little money or an injection of demand. Business only takes a breath when there is a reason to live. Business requires a bright future to endure a dark moment. Otherwise, the life in a company will slowly fade and die. Companies must have a reason to invest, hire more employees, and develop new products. A quick breath of air will only sustain a drowning business for a brief moment. The only way to sustain a business is to find products that people want not once, but again and again.

"I explained in my *Treatise* that unless the businessman makes a profit, job creation will vanish: '...wherever, by reason of the blunders of the nation or its government, production is stationary, or...the value of the product is less than the charges of its production; no productive exertion is properly rewarded; profits and wages decrease; the employment of capital becomes less advantageous and more hazardous.... The laboring classes experience a want of work; families before in tolerable circumstances, are more cramped and confined; and those before in difficulties are left altogether destitute.' (TOPE loc. 2634-83) When an economy is sick, the patient is not the consumer but the business operator. If government is to spend money to cure the economy, it should spend on things that make it easier for business to produce."

"That sounds like you're just padding the wallets of the business sector. Shouldn't government work to reduce prices or put money into the hands of consumers so they can spend more?"

"*Non.* Let me give you an example. 'During the scarcity prevalent throughout many parts of France, in the year 1775, the municipalities of Lyon and some other towns attempted to relieve the wants of the inhabitants, by buying up corn in the country, and re-selling it at a loss in the towns. To defray the expense of this operation, they at the same time obtained an increase of the *octoi* or tolls upon goods entering their gates. The scarcity grew worse and worse.'" (TOPE loc. 3660-63)

"That seems counter-intuitive. Were the tolls paid by commoners or by wealthy merchants?"

"The merchants paid, but everyone is in the system together. When government tries to extract taxes from one group, the cost is spread around until it reaches a natural level of fairness. Merchants just add the cost of paying tolls to the retail price of their products. Government cannot change prices or employment levels. Only business competition lowers prices. Only new or expanded business increases employment. Government spending is like a candle on a dark night. It is only a flash. The darkness takes no notice."

15: Multiplication Theory

"Here comes our appetizers. Jean Baptiste, I hope you will find the food in this restaurant appealing since we locals are quite proud of this place."

The wait staff places our appetizers in the center of the table and puts a square white plate and a small silver *paté* knife in front of each of us.

"*Délicieux.* Very smooth and pleasing to the tongue," says Jean Baptiste after sampling the *paté.*

"With this fuel we should be able to move our discussion forward rapidly."

"Peter, French cuisine is never fuel. It is the nectar of nature, shaped by the skilled hands of a kitchen artisan."

While Jean Baptiste waxes poetic, I glance around and notice the black widow and her black knight sitting two tables away. *This crossing of paths is too coincidental to be accidental. What is their story?*

"*Monsieur*, you look anxious. Do you want to continue with the annihilation of my nemesis?"

"You mean his ideas? I don't think that is possible, though it is a tempting thought."

"It is possible in my world."

"We are drifting away from the reality of the task." I'm grimacing now, and feel the lines in my brow sharpen.

"Back to work. What other economic totem poles do we need to topple?"

"Let's see, ten minutes ago you brushed off Keynes' idea of the multiplication of money through increased circulation. This is a topic we need to discuss thoroughly so we can make it absolutely clear to readers that without the theory of the multiplication of the money supply, deficit spending is unjustified."

Jean Baptiste says, "We have shown and history has shown that demand induced by government spending does not increase employment. The only other significant outcome of Keynes' theory is the idea that deficit spending stimulates the economy. How can we explain that situation, so it is as clear as the complexion of the woman behind you?"

Shaking my head, I ask, "Did you write your *Treatise* in a salon surrounded by beautiful women?"

"One must admit it—the angels are stimulating. Peter, you still need a good example to explain the absurdity of Keynes' multiplication theory."

"You can't think of an example?"

"You are writing for the people of your time. You need an example that excites their fancy. I have no idea what that might be."

"Okay, okay, let me think."

The waitress returns to inquire about our appetizers. I let Jean Baptiste entertain her with flattery as I ponder the perfect example to explain the flaw of Keynes' thinking about the multiplication of borrowed money.

I wake from my deep concentration to hear Jean Baptiste say, "He is fine. The bore is lost in contemplation of some obscure economic problem. Come by the next time you check on the surrounding tables. *Au revoir*." She turns her back and walks away.

"I see you got your wineglass filled. Am I also drinking wine?"

"Peter, I think it best for you to stop. You need a clear head to come up with good examples."

"Jean Baptiste, thank you so, so much for looking out for me and ensuring your wine supply is not interrupted."

"My pleasure."

"Okay, here is what I've come up with. Keynes' multiplicative theory has the horse before the cart, the withdrawal before the deposit. He requires new employment to create new savings so there will be new funds to invest. (GT p.- 117) This illustrates his failure to understand fractional banking. Banks do not need additional savings to create new funds for new investment. What banks need is assurance from the economic marketplace that additional products will find a buyer. The first point is banks need assurance from the economy that an entrepreneur will be successful. Additional savings deposits are replaced with fractional lending.

"The second point is that fractional banking is an example of the multiplicative theory in action. Keynes uses spending as an example of his multiplicative theory. Spending is not an example. Spending does not multiply or increase money. It only transfers it from one pocket to another. It is a barter exchange. The amount of money in circulation does not increase. It just moves from one hand to another. Whereas, fractional lending rules allow banks to multiply the amount of money on deposit tenfold. A one thousand dollar deposit can become a ten thousand dollar home improvement loan. This ancient process is the primary way the amount of money in society increases. The one thousand dollar cash deposit becomes a ten thousand dollar check for a new wood porch."

"Bravo, Peter. A magnificent performance, Keynes will be shocked when he reads the reviews of your performance." Our waitress looks over at us from behind a column, curious about Jean Baptiste's sudden outburst.

"Jean Baptiste, is my explanation correct?" I ask reaching for my water glass to refresh my parched mouth.

"Oui, Monsieur. You extracted the essence."

"Are you over the car alarm?"

"Oui, no permanent damage to my sanity. How do you like the Vouvray?"

"Suits me, I like the freshness of French wines. The flavors are so immediate."

"We must enjoy some more before we finish this project."

"I have another question for you. How did Keynes think the money supply would be multiplied?"

Jean Baptiste raises his gaze to the ceiling, "Keynes stated that the only way to increase investment is to lower interest rates. He believed, lower interest rates induce higher levels of investment. Higher levels of investment require the employment of more workers. More workers means more income in the community, and more income means higher consumption, which prompts yet more investment.

"Keynes looked at business investment as a mechanical process: lower interest rates and businesses will invest. It doesn't work that way. An entrepreneur makes investment decisions based on a judgment about whether a new market is opening for his goods. Without a new and lucrative market there is no new business investment."

"Let's simplify Keynes' theory. Keynes' view was that increased government spending creates a large increase in consumption. He stated that this result can be verified by looking at the increase in the consumption component of GDP before and after a government stimulus program."

"Has anyone studied the results after government stimulus injections?" asks Jean Baptiste.

"Yes, there have been thousands of studies. Milton Friedman, for instance, looked at a hundred years of GDP changes in the United States and did not find evidence of the multiplier effect. In fact, he discovered that during the Great Depression the Fed actually reduced the money supply with their high interest rate policy. His study is generally credited with clarifying that the cause of that financial calamity was regulator malfeasance. Friedman held that the Fed's actions created conditions that prolonged the Great Depression. It would be easy to show similar results during the Great Recession."

"How do modern economists isolate the numerous factors that could cause a random increase in the money supply?"

"All you can do is look at market indicators like the stock market or housing prices. Historically, during the first couple of years after a government stimulus nothing happens. Is an increase six or seven years later indicative of the stimulus money or of time and normal business activity correcting influences? No one knows."

"Am I correct that all the thousands of studies on this topic have not resolved the question of whether stimulus spending works?"

"Jean Baptiste, the entire profession is baffled except for some marginal economists that promote fringe positions. The government wants to be in control so it has been adamant in its defense of the effectiveness of deficit spending."

"But why do it," Jean Baptiste asks, "when there is no proof it works? If you borrow money, you must pay it back. It appears to me that the case for not borrowing is much stronger."

"I agree, but the government finds itself in a difficult position because it wants to do something."

"Is it possible that doing nothing is the best action?"

"It could be. The only time it was tried was in 1987 by President Reagan."

"And what happened?"

"Nothing. In six months the stock market was back to where it was before the crash."

"What? Why have governments continued to follow a path in the opposite direction? Such dogmatic ineptitude is criminal. People should be guillotined, not excused for making a policy error. This is the kind of nonsense we must correct."

In the midst of this crescendo of emotion, our entrees arrive. Jean Baptiste slumps back into his chair and accepts his dinner, like a homeless person getting an ice cream scoop of mashed potatoes. I also feel dazed.

Our waitress returns shortly after the service is complete. She walks up behind Jean Baptiste, wraps her arms around his shoulders, and whispers in his ear, "How does that look, *Monsieur*?"

"*Mademoiselle*, it looks lovely, but it is the taste that matters."

"True, but it is the beauty that draws your attention."

"*Oui*, and my attention is drawn."

She says, "Gentlemen, enjoy this culinary interlude of the best of Parisian culture in Portland."

"*Mademoiselle*, we shall, we shall."

"Thank you," I say.

Jean Baptiste takes his spoon and dips in for a taste of his egg and spinach custard. "We still must dispel Keynes' idea of the fiscal multiplier."

Stunned by Jean Baptiste's immediate return to economics, I hesitate before responding, "I suppose, to begin, we should clarify the difference between Keynes' fiscal multiplier and the monetary multiplier of fractional lending. I assume that you agree with me that the monetary multiplier is real and highly effective."

"*Oui*, I think we should make that argument. It is also a multiplier outside the government's corrupt hand and inside the market."

"Jean Baptiste, we need to avoid hyperbole if our arguments are to be accepted and respected."

"Absurd."

I don't reply. I know that he'll be civil for the sake of the book, but still be a beast around his friends."

"The standard definition of Keynes' fiscal multiplier is a change in national income related to an increase in spending by the national government," I say.

"Obviously, if more money is spent on federal projects the total amount of in the money supply will increase, but that does not lead to more job creation or economic growth," Jean Baptiste asserts. "Imagine if all employees are given a raise. No new employees are hired. And all the employees use their raise to pay off debts. No new business is stimulated."

"That is exactly what happened when President Bush rebated three hundred dollars to every low and moderate income taxpayers in 2008 as part of a stimulus bill at the beginning of the Great Recession. No multiplier effect was detected. None."

Jean Baptiste concludes, "Keynes' multiplier is an assumed psychological effect, but your example shows that it does not always occur."

"Also," I say, "basing economic policy on the total amount spent in an economy is foolish. It is not connected to the success of society or a business. A used car lot operator might lower his prices to attract more customers. For the first three months he might quadruple his sales, but lose money every day. After three months of record sales, the company closes and the employees are laid off."

"Total spending is not an indicator of economic health, but tax receipts might be," Jean Baptiste suggests. "How about taking total tax receipts and dividing by tax expenditures to get a sense of economic health."

"For the ratio to be meaningful, everything would have to be held constant: tax policy, population, etc. But the ratio of tax revenue to total government spending might be a good indicator. Tax revenue reflects economic vitality in all sectors, and captures the effect of unemployment and business stagnation. The denominator, by including government stimulus spending as part of the total, captures all government spending. Yeah, I like it."

"Do you think it would capture multiplier effects?" asked Jean Baptiste.

"There is a great movie called *Ghostbusters* in which a device is used to eliminate ghosts by sucking them up like a vacuum cleaner."

"That's a horrible thought!"

"I was just trying to make a comparison to your tax revenue index. It doesn't matter if ghosts or Keynes' multiplier effect are real or not. If no signs of ghosts are detected when the machine stops, the problem is solved. Similarly, the multiplier effect will be incorporated in the ratio whether it is real or not. But it is foolish to make government policy based on an effect that cannot be observed."

"We also need to factor inflation into the formula."

"I got it, boss."

Jean Baptiste suddenly looks down at his plate as if seeing it for the first time. "We should eat our food before it spoils."

"I agree, though I have been taking a spoonful every now and then during your rants."

"Peter, I am concerned about your lack of seriousness and passion."

16: Celebrity Spokesman

"Excuse me? What's wrong with my passion?"

"You lack the fire necessary to sell an idea."

"How's that possible? Economics is my whole life. It's what I do to earn a living. It's what I think about day and night."

"I am not saying you are not dedicated, but I cannot feel your heart. You seem too dry, too analytical. An economic theory needs red hot passion to flow from the pulpit and ignite the spirits in the congregation. My theory needs a dynamic spokesman, not an accountant. Sorry."

"Does this mean you're giving up on me? I can't believe you suddenly have these reservations. What did I do or say?"

"Nothing in particular; it is just a realization that struck me. You are not the right flag bearer. I need someone people will rally around and support."

"You think you need a celebrity?" I say. "Well, you don't. It's your ideas that will attract people. A celebrity will just split your audience between the celebrity's fans and detractors. It will no longer be about your ideas."

"Peter, do not be upset. Personal charisma is important when selling ideas."

"Jean Baptiste, you are not selling makeup. Don't you see a distinction between beauty products and the world of ideas? Do you want someone taking your serious efforts to reform society and turning them into a soap opera?"

"Peter, let us finish our dinner and continue this outside. I need a puff."

"Oh my God, I can't believe this... Maybe it is time to move on."

"Compose yourself. You can convince me to change my mind," Jean Baptiste says with assurance.

"How can I do that? It sounds like your mind is closed. I took two days out of my busy life just to hear that I might not be a good fit? This is outrageous. Why did I drive up here? Just to be embarrassed?"

Jean Baptiste picks up his silverware, piles everything beside his plate, and raises his arm to get our waitress' attention. We settle our bill and walk outside in silence.

Two steps outside the restaurant entry Jean Baptiste pulls his pipe out of his coat pocket.

"You can't light up here. Let's get away from the traffic. Follow me." I lead him around the corner to Salmon Street and we walk up to the Park Blocks then turn north in the direction of both the Benson and my hotel.

"Peter, are you upset with me?"

"What was your first clue?"

"I do not understand your attitude. I thought you were committed, like me, to having the world adopt the proper economic principles. We have a chance to correct an egregious error. Why are you walking away?"

"Just a second here, it's not me who is walking away! You rejected my help, not five minutes ago."

"Peter, we must have the right spokesman. Why not help me find the right speaker instead of throwing a tantrum?"

"Oh my God, the author of the book is insignificant. The focus needs to be on the ideas included in the book. I may not be the greatest writer on planet Earth, but I'm adequate for this task. You don't need a Pulitzer Prize-winning author. You need someone who can elucidate an idea."

"I was not impressed with your dance around an example to dispute Keynes' multiplier theory."

"Holy cow, is that what this is about?" I look at Jean Baptiste as he stands with his back to the deserted Park Blocks, pipe sagging from his mouth, inhaling smoke through his nose and pulling on each sleeve in turn. "You are probably right. Let me sleep on it. I will come up with an example."

"I would like that."

We proceed down the Park Blocks.

That was an uncomfortable moment. He appears totally unaware of the distress his comments caused me. Why have I become so completely invested in this project? I suppose it's because I do believe it has merit. Ideas are extremely powerful and the proper economic idea could change the future from a dismal prospect to an appealing destination.

I speed up to close the gap between us, "Jean Baptiste, I respect your passion, but what is it about this book that makes you so driven?"

"Pete, it is not the book. It is the need to right a wrong."

"Clarify for me, what is that wrong again?"

"Government should not be in control of the economy, consumers should."

"Okay, I get that, but what's the harm?"

"I knew you were distracted. All day we have been discussing the harm."

Head down, looking at the sidewalk, I recall the purpose of the day. "I wasn't distracted. We've spent the day discussing various aspects of Keynes' theory...to show that an economic system managed by government is...inefficient, shallow, and artificial. Oh, I get it." I look up and see Jean Baptiste smiling.

"Peter, are you concerned about people?"

"Of course I am."

"In fact, you care deeply about people. Richard told me you did. That is why I sought you out. Keynes cared most about himself and his job. His theory is a justification for state power. The intent of his theory was not to help people better their lives. The purpose of his theory was to secure his authority. That is why I want to correct his theory."

"You played me!"

"I just wanted to be sure, because I cannot stay around much more to help you. Tomorrow may be my last day with you. What is this ahead of us? Is it a market?"

I look up and see we are approaching the Alder Street food trucks. I gather my thoughts before replying. *The old dude–the really old dude–is wise, really wise. Now what was his question?*

I gather myself and reply, "These are mini-restaurants built inside of trucks. Every variety of food is served. You just go up to the window, give them your order, and they cook everything in a kitchen inside the truck. Some of the best Thai food in the city is served from these trucks."

"The way the trucks are lined up on the perimeter of the square reminds me of the caravan markets that would visit French villages during the summer. That must bring a smile to crotchety-old Jean Baptiste. "Were the markets in France small restaurants?"

"*Non*, they were selling goods and crafts. Many were gypsies who traveled north during the summer to sell goods, tell fortunes, sharpen knives, collect metal scrap, or trade horses. They often lived in their carts. Some carts had a smokestack like these food trucks connected to a small stove for heating and cooking. Sorry for the interruption. The vision of these trucks and the people gathered about just reminded me of my homeland."

"It is amazing how slowly some things change," I comment, "like the wisdom of the ages."

"It is equally amazing how rapidly other things change," says Jean Baptiste. "In my lifetime, I saw the first stores placed inside buildings. Now, it is common for retail stores to be located in buildings built solely for that purpose, but when I was born all retail trade was transacted outside on the town square."

I can't resist adding, "In the brief 200 years that separate us, the primary energy of commerce has changed from horsepower to the gasoline engine."

"Life is brief. Your life will last a 100 years about half the 200 years that separates us, but not as long as our ideas."

"Your ideas. I'm only a scribe."

Jean Baptiste looks at me paternally. "By the time you are finished writing this book the ideas will be yours."

"I don't know about that, but I'll do everything possible to be true to your beliefs."

"Embrace the ideas we develop as your own or your passion will be hollow. An empty heart cannot circulate the truth necessary for your ideas to succeed. I am getting tired. Are we far from the

Benson? I just want to get back and have a brandy and go to sleep."

"The Benson is just down this hill. I'll walk you to the front door. Tomorrow I'll pick you up at 8 a.m. for breakfast at a place that specializes in the morning fare."

"With a delicious breakfast feast awaiting my awakening, I will sleep soundly."

17: Strength of Assumptions

I drop Jean Baptiste off at his hotel, then retrace my steps back up the hill on Stark Street toward my reserved bed at the Crystal Hotel about four blocks away. The Crystal is located on the upper floors of a three-building triangular block. The lobby is located in a building that was originally the Hotel Alma, built in 1911. *I wonder if the old hotel building has a ghostly past.*

When the Automobile Age dawned, the hotel and storefronts were converted to car related businesses. This location on the most heavily traveled street to the west of downtown was visible to the commuting population. The area quickly became Portland's Auto Row. This was a time when a car dealership had a single show window and only one or two cars on the premises.

As times changed so did the use of these buildings. The street level of the former Hotel Alma was opened up to become one of the first drive-through banks in Portland, a convenient way for new automobile drivers to pay their monthly auto financing bills. The Automobile Age owes its development as much to some anonymous credit manager as to Henry Ford.

This particular drive-through was designed by Portland's most heralded architect, Pietro Belluschi. Sixty years later Mr. Belluschi would design the then-tallest building in Portland, "Big Pink," the home of U.S. Bank, a company built on auto and business lending.

The next evolution of this triangular block was as a series of nightclubs in the 1940s. One of the most notorious owners was "Half-World" Al Winter who had one foot in legitimate companies and the other in the underworld. His notoriety originated when he joined up with Bugsy Siegel, Mickey Cohen, and Meyer Lansky to open the Sahara Hotel and Casino in Las Vegas. Sometime later, competing nightclub owner Nathan Zusman was asked to appear before the Senate Committee on Racketeering, headed by Robert Kennedy. Washington DC shone the spotlight on the Portland block but never dimmed the neon lights. Gradually, the block embraced the 1960s and the lower floor became a head shop, *The Free People's Touching Company.*

In the late 1970s the block became the center of the gay community, which was fixated on the nightclub scene at Stark Street Station, Bushes, Flossies, and Silverado. By the 1980s at the annual Stark Street Fair, organized by Stephen Boden aka

Flossie, had become a gay pride event, the first of its kind in Portland.

At the turn of the 21st century, the McMenamin clan purchased the triangle block and converted it into a brew pub-hotel-restaurant complex. I like the place, because it is a cheap date among the downtown hotels. There is a reason for that: pets, the animal kind, are allowed in the rooms. In an old building with gaps in the structure, dog sounds make their way from canine room to canine room. This produces a surround-sound cacophony that prevents any kind of human sleep. Techniques such as head hiding under three pillows, sleeping at the bottom of the bed buried under two bed covers, pushing fingers on foam ear plugs or soaking a brain in alcohol do nothing to silence the noise. The latter is the most popular method, but believe me, it doesn't work—not even close.

Sometimes in the middle of the night the desk clerk arrives and slides a dog dish filled with a shot of vodka under the door. Two minutes later, all is quiet on the western front.

I walk into the lobby. Quarterflash, Portland's own two hit wonder, is blasting from the sound system: *'Find another fool to love you. Find another fool to love you.'*

I wonder if I should have tried that line on Jean Baptiste?

The desk clerk greets me, shouting over the music. "Good evening, Mr. Barrie. I have located you to a room that I think you will find quieter than your last visit." He hands me a new set of keys and tells me I am now in Room 308. I thank him and head up to my new room, called "Lazy Eye" after the hit recording by the group, *Silversun Pickups*. Every room is named after a rock'n'roll song. The theme is carried into the room with art pieces that relate to the song or the group that performed it. Usually there is a period photo of the group performing at the nearby Crystal Palace concert hall, after which the hotel is named.

Amazing place. It has a vaudeville aesthetic that harkens back to the over-the-top gay stage shows performed at Flossies and Silverado in the neighborhood. The colors of the halls, painted with diagonal stripes, diamonds, or chevrons, are burgundy, big top ochre, and starry night blue. The corridors are barely lit by a random collection of different colored bulbs peeking out from Victorian style hanging fixtures with pressed glass shades in soothing tones. This light fixture aesthetic continues into the rooms where the location of each light is governed by the same laws that govern stalactites arrangement in caves.

In "Lazy Eye" there is an eye painted high on the wall opposite the bed, keeping watch on all the activity in the room. I stare carefully, trying to see if the pupil is a painted black dot or a dark cavity. I can't tell. I do notice the eye blink, but only once.

It is still early so I decide to go down to the pool before attempting to sleep. I'm still energized by my conversation with Jean Baptiste.

I slip on my bathing suit and wrap myself in a large robe I find on a hook behind the door. I take the elevator down to the basement and enter the pool room. It's not a swimming pool, but a 100-degree soaking pool.

I walk in at the end of the pool where hot water plunges from huge bronze spouts into the long pond. The walls are paneled in bamboo and the bath is overseen by a stern Babylonian official in bronze. The room is very dark except for the dramatic underwater lighting in the pool. The most dramatic element is the sculptural edge of the pool deck, which is neither straight nor curved but follows a long arabesque line, giving the space a Middle Eastern ambiance. The heat radiating from the pool and the steam obscuring the view all add to the mysterious ambience. The perfect place to review my day with the enigmatic Mr. Say.

I place my robe and towel on a hook and slip into the water. The heat is a challenge, but irresistibly soothing to my stiff muscles. I lie against the side of the pool and let my legs and feet float, until I am supported only by my head as it rests on the pool perimeter. I began to feel like a Babylonian official, soaking the day's dust off.

"Excuse me."

Christ, who the hell is that?

I open my eyes and bend my head back to see the upside down boyfriend of the black widow bending down behind me. "Yes?" I spit out.

"Sorry to bother you, sir, but I noticed you today at a number of the venues we were visiting."

"Yes, you look somewhat familiar," I answer coldly without a tinge of honesty.

"We saw you first at Olde Towne Pizza, then at Lan Su Chinese Garden, and a couple of hours ago at the Heathman."

"Who is 'we'?"

"I refer to my associate, Helga. Helga, come join us."

Did he say 'Hell gate'? So the confrontation is going to occur in the water and I left my spear gun in my room.

Helga approaches, "Yes, I recall seeing you today. How can I help you?"

"This is Helga and I am Fritz. We are German travel writers and we are doing a piece on Portland."

Mystery solved, and without bloodshed. Thank God, I didn't want to attract sharks.

Helga kneels down onto the pool deck and reaches her hand out to me. *"Gutentag."*

I take her hand. "Glad to meet you. I am Peter, Peter Barrie. I'm from California, just visiting Portland for a couple of days."

"Oh, we will go to California later this week," says Fritz. "We are working on an itinerary for our last couple of days here in Portland, and I would like to ask you a few questions, if you do not object."

"Sure, but I'm no expert. Go ahead, ask away."

"One of the places we want to visit is the *Women and Women First Bookstore*..."

I interrupt, "From the *Portlandia* TV show?"

"Ja, they show it in Deutschland."

"Is that how you learned about Portland?"

"Nein, we did research, but the TV show got us interested. Portlandians are like us, but only after we get a few beers in our bellies."

"Are Germans that obsessive?"

"Ja, sometimes, especially about work."

"That is quite different from the people in Portland. They're obsessive about how they act."

"*Ja*, that is why we want to find the bookstore. Is it not one of the centers of the Portlandia culture?"

"It probably is, although the TV producers changed the name. It's over on the east side, on Hawthorne. The real name is In Other Words. You can look it up."

"*Ja*, we can do that. Do you know where the Quilted Tea Kettle Inn is located?"

"No. I think that is a made-up place, but I'm not sure."

"Do you know where Jackpot Records is located?"

"Again, I'm not sure, but it might be based on the record store on Burnside that is next to Powell's Books."

"Can I ask you one last question? Does the mayor in his office sit on a red ball?"

Can I resist? "Don't all men?"

"Oh my!" Helga responds.

"You have a continental sense of humor," says Fritz.

"I'll take that as a compliment."

"*Danke shehr*. We appreciate the help."

"Glad to be of assistance."

Peter, you shouldn't judge people by their costumes.

Alone in the pool, I scold myself for jumping to conclusions about Fritz and Helga—just two young travel writers trying to make their way in a difficult field. *I would have enjoyed talking to them about their writing experiences. Unfortunately, I lost that opportunity by copping an attitude about two people. Shameful, and here I am expecting people to embrace a new economic approach from an economist hundreds of years removed from their reality.*

Disappointed in myself, I decide to leave the hot pool and return to my room and work on my sleep deficit. I climb out of the water, dry off, and return to my room.

I hang up my towel and bathrobe, then remove from the bed the three unmatched pillows: an animal print with lavender spots, a faux leather circle pillow, and a black velvet arabesque patterned one. I take my clothes off the bed and dress a chair beside the window hanging my coat jacket from the back and draping my pants over the seat. As I walk away it looks like a thin man melted into the chair. Its location seemingly calculated by a diabolically eccentric interior designer to ensure a middle of the night fright to all insecure guests, of which I am one.

I have nothing to fear at the moment, though, because the dogs throughout the hotel scare away all the ghosts and goblins until about 2 a.m. The noise wasn't that bad. It was only noticeable when you laid your head on your pillow and tried to sleep.

I spent a fitful night in "Lazy Eye" enduring dog wailing. In the morning I suggest to the desk clerk that they change the name of my room to "Baggy Eyes" by the country group, *My Grains*.

"Sorry. We had a couple of dogs who stayed out late partying last night."

"The problem was that they brought the party back to their rooms."

"I am sorry about that. Occasionally some dogs have a hard time winding down. Can we offer you a coupon for a free drink at Stumptown Coffee to soothe your awakening?"

"Can you post a sign outside the dog run on the roof that there's no wailing at the moon after midnight?"

"We will do better than that. We will ask the dog owners to silence their dogs, or allow us to relocate them to the soundproof room in the basement," replies the desk clerk, posing as a truant officer with the requisite Air Force mirrored sunglasses and a scowl of disapproval.

Satisfied with this display of human power over dog impertinence, and with my free cup of coffee coupon, I walk outside and over to Stumptown Coffee.

18: Summing up

Stumptown Coffee is packed with people silently conversing with their open silver colored Apple MACs. Feeling slightly out of place without a MAC, I leave Stumptown Coffee. I walk down to the Benson to pick up Jean Baptiste for breakfast. We meet in the lobby and saunter seven blocks downhill to Mother's Bistro and Bar. Michelle has not yet arrived.

The restaurant has a 1960s suburban kitchen ambience, with glossy acrylic white bead board walls—easy to clean. The waitress stations are constructed from standard residential white upper and lower cabinets. Above the top row of cabinets and behind the cornice is a collection of colorful antique milk pitchers. The wait staff dresses in all-white with white kitchen aprons tied on and a white hand towel tucked in at the waist.

The maître' de leads us to a table on the perimeter of a large room, next to the windows.

The view outside is obscured by delicate filigree drapes but the room is bright and cheery, like the morning in a French sunroom.

"Peter, I like this place," says Jean Baptiste.

"I do too. I hope Michelle didn't run into a problem. I didn't speak to her this morning. I neglected to call her."

"I am sure she will be along soon. Shall we order coffee and a pastry while we wait?"

"Good idea. Here comes our waitress now."

"Good morning, gentlemen. Here are your menus. Can I start you off with coffees?"

"*Oui*, I will have a *café au lait* and a *croissant*."

Turning to me, "How about you, sir?"

"I will have the same thing, but can I get a little powdered sugar and cinnamon sprinkled on my croissant?"

"Absolutely. Anything else at this time?"

"No, that will wake us up."

"Peter, what is on the schedule for today?"

"Let's wait until Michelle arrives to discuss that. In the meantime, we should discuss the topics in our book more completely. The discussion of Keynesian flaws we covered yesterday is fine, but I think we need to give the reader a complete description of the components of your replacement theory."

"I agree," says Jean Baptiste. "The book must fill the vacuum that will be created when Keynesian economics is invalidated. Where should we start?"

"By refuting Keynes' description of your views with his so-called Say's Law."

"That is where Keynes struck the first blow. We need to knock him off his high horse, overturn his equestrian statue in front of Parliament, lop off his head, and release his horse to do something noble. Remember, that is the point of the book!"

"Okay, okay. This is where the book should begin, but I want to outline an economic direction people can use in their nation's economic system. Don't you agree?"

Jean Baptiste is still breathing deeply as his blackened lungs try to recover from the challenge of the walk to the restaurant. "*Oui, Monsieur.*"

"I'm confident that you have given me enough to prove the IS/LM model is incorrect. Entrepreneurs do not manage their businesses to maximize the profit they can make from each employee. Instead, they choose new niches and expansion opportunities based on market conditions. So focusing on taxing the rich or creating new government jobs is exactly the wrong approach for restoring the economy. We need to look at the market conditions for entrepreneurs, for consumers, and for suppliers and try to make them more efficient."

"Peter, I agree."

Our waitress approaches, "Gentlemen, may I serve your coffees? They were prepared by our coffee stewards with a Costa Rican bean in a French press. And here are your croissants."

"Thank you. It looks delicious," I say. Jean Baptiste is already sipping his *café au lait*.

"To continue, I also have enough information about the differences between the kind of top-down government directed economy that Keynes preferred and your preference for a market directed economy."

"Pete, the book should distinguish between Keynes' theory of economic management as a tool for social modification and my theory of the economy as a machine for societal wealth creation."

"I agree. We must emphasize that Keynes felt there was an ideal social arrangement that could be described in an economic model and that, among other feats of incredible strength and endurance, would encourage employment and stabilize prices. In fact, didn't Keynes believe the purpose of economics was to discover this model?"

"*Oui*, and that is one of the most misused aspects of his theory. It has led us on a search as futile as Ponce de Leon's quest for the Fountain of Youth and as destructive as John Law's issuance of unbacked monetary notes."

"It will make our case if we can prove that trying to model an economy mathematically is a futile endeavor."

"The best we can do is state that it is impossible to predict the behavior of dynamic, unpredictable humankind with an inert mathematical model. People are often irrational and creative in ways unforeseen in a formula. But if any of our readers are persons mesmerized by the magic of crystal balls, or the undecipherable mathematical formulas of academics, then we cannot convince them of the obvious."

"Jean Baptiste, those types of statements will be especially powerful when we support them with some of your other complementary ideas."

"I hope so."

Over Jean Baptiste's shoulder, I notice Michelle enter and look for us. I raise my arm to signal her. She smiles broadly and waves her arm.

Her enthusiasm makes me smile. "Michelle has arrived."

Jean Baptiste pushes his chair back and half turns to face the entry. "She looks beautiful."

Michelle has her black glossy hair tied back in a ponytail. She is wearing little makeup, but her eyes stand out, beaming with happiness as she approaches.

Jean Baptiste casts an eye over Michelle's entire outfit: high black heels and tight black leggings beneath a long loose-fitting red cashmere sweater, tightly tied gray scarf around her neck. "*Mademoiselle*, you are a delight for old tired eyes."

"Thank you, Jean Baptiste, but did you not sleep well?"

"I slept soundly, but I have spent a lifetime looking at a world of narcissistic strivers more interested in their personal importance than solving world problems. It is a tiring task I have given myself."

"We all thank you for your sacrifice. Don't we, Peter?"

"Oh yes," I reply.

"Have I missed breakfast?"

"Oh no, *Mademoiselle*, we were waiting your arrival. We can order now." Jean Baptiste hands Michelle a menu. "We did have a *café au lait* and a *croissant* while waiting, but the main course awaits."

"I'll pass on the croissant, but the coffee sounds wonderful. What are you going to have for breakfast?"

I see my chance to squeeze into the conversation. "I recommend the cheddar cheese scramble with pork sausage infused with fennel."

"That sounds perfect. I was up early to study and haven't had a thing to eat. Jean Baptiste, are you going to join us with the scramble?"

"It sounds a bit British, but I am feeling adventuresome. Count me in."

A moment later our waitress comes to take our order and bring a hot coffee for Michelle.

"What were you scholars discussing when I arrived?"

"Pete, I have forgotten. What were we talking about?"

"One topic we waited to discuss until you arrived is our program for the day."

"Are you accepting recommendations?"

"Oui, Mademoiselle."

"I think you would enjoy the Japanese Garden. It is rated one of the best in the United States."

"It sounds delightful, dear."

"That's a winner even during the preamble to winter," I comment. "And how about something technological like the Portland Streetcar or the light rail?"

"Or the Oregon Health Sciences University cable car? It is much more exciting than a couple of commuter trains. Jean Baptiste, are you bored with trains?" asks Michelle.

"*Non*, railways were just beginning when I passed in 1832. I never saw one. Most were in England."

"Okay, that's one possibility," I note.

Michelle adds, "If we take the cable car up to OHSU we can visit the Edmund Starr Dental Museum. Jean Baptiste, do you like grotesque teeth?"

"*Non*, not an interest of mine."

"His interest might bend more to the Hat Museum or Stark's Vacuum Museum," I propose.

"What is in a vacuum museum?"

"Nothing. You didn't read any books on vacuums in your visits to the Paris library?" Michelle teases. "A vacuum is a household appliance for picking dirt off the floor."

Jean Baptiste frowns.

"Okay, how 'bout the Hat Museum?" I inquire. "Any interest in seeing the variety of hats people wore in the last couple of hundred years?"

"That does not sound interesting. I prefer the Japanese Garden. It must be a pleasant place to stroll and converse."

"It is the perfect place for strolling," says Michelle. "Peter, we can catch the light rail line on First and then transfer to the Portland Streetcar to take us to 23rd just below the Japanese Garden. From there we can get a taxi to take us into Washington Park."

"Great idea, Michelle," I say. "Jean Baptiste can experience all our major forms of transportation in one trip. How does that sound?"

"That would complete my day," he says.

Our breakfast arrives while we're talking, and with our plans for the day settled, everyone digs in.

19 : Do Expenditures Matter?

Outside the cozy confines of Mother's Bistro, Jean Baptiste lights up and leaves a trail of pungent smoke as we walk the two blocks to the light rail stop. We wait for the train. The entire street is empty except for the occasional car. The only smell is Jean Baptiste's pipe. The lack of urban noise makes me uncomfortable. When the train arrives silently from behind us, Jean Baptiste reacts to its sudden appearance in his peripheral vision by raising his arms as if a rifle barrel had suddenly been shoved against his back. His reaction sends the contents of his pipe up into the air. Recovering, he kicks the remains into the gutter.

"*Sacre bleu*, that was a surprise," he says, tapping his pipe bowl against the heel of his shoe.

I climb on the train and reach back to assist Jean Baptiste, "Come on, step up here, and hurry," I advise as I take hold of the post inside the train and I reach back to help him aboard. Outside on the sidewalk, Michelle slips her arm under his and directs him onto the first step.

"I am coming, I am coming!" he says. Once on board we find seats facing each other across the aisle.

"Jean Baptiste, we get off at the next stop. We will do the exact opposite of what we did to get on. Be ready." I can tell from his pasty face that he is struggling to remember what just happened. "This is just a short ride, but we will have more time to savor the experience on the next leg. Here we are."

Jean Baptiste cautiously exits the train. He seems more relieved than excited by the experience. I can't resist saying, "Are you ready to do it again?" My sarcasm is not received favorably by the audience.

Michelle takes Jean Baptiste's hand, "The streetcar is much slower and we will sit beside a window to watch the city pass."

"Am I safe in these things?"

I quickly respond, "Safer than on the streets."

"Peter, stop it. You're scaring him. Jean Baptiste, it is perfectly safe. I take the streetcar and light rail all over Portland. Let me help you on and off."

While the two Francophiles bond, I go over to the ticket machine and buy three yellow day-passes for the streetcar. As I walk back, I see the streetcar make its way toward us, hugging the ground like a creeping slug. We board without incident and ride up to 23rd Avenue. When we are safely back on the sidewalk I ask, "Was that a memorable experience?"

Confidence restored, Jean Baptiste answers smartly, "*Oui*, I like the steady, smooth motion. Riding in a carriage pulled by horses is jarring, although the silence of the streetcar is unsettling."

"Oh yes, the electric motors only make a slight whirring sound."

We board an electric Prius for the taxi ride up to the Japanese Garden, and Jean Baptiste takes in the experience like a seasoned traveler. The taxi drops us off and we walk up the last of the roadway to the entry.

I raise my arm and circle my hand to indicate everything around us. "Jean Baptiste, all of this is part of Washington Park, an immense public reserve that includes the International Rose Test Garden we just drove through, the Oregon Zoo, the Portland Children's Museum, the Pittock Mansion that we may visit if we have time, and the Japanese Garden."

"The Japanese Garden is my favorite," says Michelle.

"*Mademoiselle*, I am excited to visit it. In Paris we have a large park named the *Tuileries*."

"Why was it named that?"

"The land was used by roof tile makers before the monarchy acquired the land for the Park. The *Tuileries* garden was opened to the public during holidays such as the Feast Day of Saint Louis. The monarchy paid for free concerts and fireworks. Like your Alder Street food carts, there were food stalls inside the grounds and chairs could be rented to sit and enjoy the natural surroundings."

"That sounds pleasant, but isn't the *Tuileries* palace where King Louis the Sixteenth and Queen Marie Antoinette spent their last days?"

"*Oui*, the mob stormed the palace and took them to be guillotined. Their Swiss guards were chased through the garden and killed."

"Oh, gruesome history."

"*Mademoiselle*, it was only a single day. By the 18th century the *Tuileries* was the place all of Paris came to experience nature, to stroll, socialize, and relax."

"It sounds like you favor large public works," I remark.

Jean Baptiste lowers his eyebrows at me. "The monarchy used parks like the emperors of Rome used the coliseum—as places to celebrate their glory and pacify the masses."

"Okay, but what is your personal view of government collecting taxes for large public works?"

"I believe I made that perfectly clear in my Treatise: 'Government expenditures [end up] lost to the world.'" (TOPE loc. 8659)

"Can you explain why that is?"

Jean Baptiste shakes his head in irritation. "There is a fundamental difference between government expenditures and business expenditures. Expenditures for a farmer are seed, fertilizer, and food for horses. Expenditures for the state are the same: food for troops, tents, weapons, etc. The result of the farmer's purchases is a product that can be sold to purchase more seed, fertilizer, food for horses and profit to be used to purchase products for his home. There is no profit that results from the state's expenditures. The government must collect taxes to pay for these same items the next year."

"That statement from your *Treatise* has always bothered me, but now I get it."

"What statement is that, Peter?" asks Michelle.

"That government expenditures are lost to the world."

Michelle bites her lower lip. "I'm still confused. The money spent to purchase a rifle goes to the rifle manufacturer, and he makes a profit, doesn't he?"

"Yes," I say, "but in the farmer example, both the farmer and the seed supplier make profits. In the military example, the army does not make a profit, only the rifle manufacturer. Government is an economically neutral step. There is no economic advantage to having the state purchase the rifle. Using the government is a lost opportunity for someone in society to make a profit."

"Jean Baptiste, is he right?"

"*Oui, Mademoiselle*, I said it even stronger in my *Treatise*: 'Taxes take wealth out of a community.' (TOPE loc. 9127) Once that money is in the state's hands it does not create new business or additional profits in the community."

The sun begins to cut through the morning fog, and Michelle takes off her sweater and scarf. She shakes her clingy ponytail to lay it gently on her now bare shoulders, and says, "So during the time that tax money is in government hands it does not contribute to the growth of the economy, but once given to a soldier as salary it returns to the economy. Is that the gist of your idea?"

Jean Baptiste takes on the role of professor: "That is largely correct, but the public money spent to maintain this elaborate garden proves my point that 'public expenditures do not recycle'." (TOPE loc. 8064) If the same money were used to maintain a factory, that expenditure would generate a profit each year—over and over."

"It's not about money disappearing, but about making money work to keep the economy growing and continuing to produce," I add.

Sensing that Michelle is satisfied with the account, Jean Baptiste concludes, "If you understand those concepts then you can understand that capital should be employed where the greatest profit occurs.' (TOPE loc 7049). That happens in the business sector, not the government sector."

I say, "Michelle, this argument shows that making government expenditures to lift the economy out of a slump, as Keynes advised, is less effective than private investment. All commerce is a barter exchange unless there is a profit involved. Because they fail to maximize profit opportunities, government expenditures are the worst possible course to correct an economic slump."

"Wow, I wish my professors could explain economics like you two!"

"*Mademoiselle*, you are too kind."

"I'm just glad we can find the words to describe a better path than Keynesian economics," I reply.

As we approach the Japanese Garden, Jean Baptiste says, "This is a magnificent entry gate. I am ready to see more."

We buy our tickets and enter the five-acre garden, one of the premier Japanese gardens outside of Japan.

Michelle acts as our guide. "A Japanese garden is composed of three materials: rock, water and plants. Rocks provide the structure for the garden. Water is the life-giving force. Plants are the time element, revealing the season."

"The use of plants is quite different from French gardens," Jean Baptiste says. "Plants provide the structure in our gardens. We have more concrete and cut stone than rocks. Rocks provide decorative touches such as beneath waterfalls."

"In this garden there are five distinctly different styles: the Flat Garden, the Strolling Pond Garden, the Tea Garden, the Natural Garden, and the Sand and Stone Garden. Come up this way and we'll visit the Flat Garden first."

Michelle leads us up the walk to a large pavilion and then up a couple of stairs onto the veranda at the back. We look out on a vast plain of raked white gravel surrounded on three sides by plantings primarily of azalea and low-growing pines. The raked white gravel is striking, and effective in creating an illusion of a pond, with the plantings in the distance as a plausible green shoreline. The scale of the plantings perfectly supports the illusion.

Michelle says, "Jean Baptiste, can you see how the garden designer rearranged common elements from nature in a harmonious way? The shoreline is realistic, but it undulates up and down and back and forth in an appealing rhythm."

"*Mademoiselle*, it is beautiful and soothing. I like it. It is quite unlike the geometric arrangement of European gardens. Our gardens are about controlling nature. This garden is about extolling nature."

"Well said. Gentlemen, stroll about and enjoy the views. Go inside the pavilion and see how the Shoji screens frame the garden. It looks like there is also a display of Ikebana inside to enjoy. When you are ready to move on, meet me at the bottom of the stairs over there," says Michelle, pointing to the steps at the other end of the veranda.

She turns and walks into the pavilion. Her movement pushes a cloud of fragrance through the opening. Jean Baptiste and I inhale; we look at each other and decide to follow her.

I open a screen for Jean Baptiste to walk through, and as I turn to close it my attention is caught by a large group of women and girls strolling up the path. The older women look at each other, the young women are engrossed by the complex beauty of their surroundings, and the young girls hurry to see what is next. *Age changes perceptions.*

A similar group of men and boys follow the females. The old men peer deeply into the garden rooms, under and around clumps of rhododendrons and azaleas, across carpets of moss, into tangles of branches, looking for details missed by their companions. *Looking for something to comment on.* The young men look right and left as if hunting for prey. I awake from my observational stupor and follow Jean Baptiste inside.

I walk along a long table of flower arrangements that are entries in a competition.

After a few moments I hear, "Peter, are you ready to go?" Michelle and Jean Baptiste walk past me and back onto the veranda and down the exit steps. I turn and follow.

"Let's walk through the Natural Garden and meet in the Sand and Stone Garden for some serious reflection. Or Peter, have you had your fill of reflection?"

"I certainly drifted off," I say.

We walk down the hill on a series of granite steps, some cut and others just natural flat pieces laid to form a pathway. The path turns sharply to avoid rock outcrops and large boulders in the hillside. The arrangement of the steps and the density of the plantings creates a more enclosed environment, very different from the open sunny Flat Garden. Michelle puts her sweater back on.

At the bottom of the hill we come to the Sand and Stone Garden. Michelle says, "This is a traditional dry garden with raked sand surrounding three carefully selected rocks inside a walled sanctuary. The sand is raked in a series of concentric rings around each rock to represent waves being deflected off a rocky shoreline. Typically called a Zen garden, this type of garden represents the beauty of blank space. These gardens are often found in Zen temple compounds, where they are used by the monks to contemplate the universe."

"Jean Baptiste, we should seek guidance from the universe before we continue our challenging search for economic truth," I say.

He and I stand silently, looking at the garden and observing the relationship of the rocks to each other and the universe. In the moment just before enlightenment, our guide says, "Scholars, we must move on. The best is at the top of the hill. Just follow the signs to the Strolling Pond Garden. I'll meet you at the Koi pond." She turns and flies up the hill.

There is no flying up the hill for Jean Baptiste and me. I look at him and give a deep sigh. He looks up the hill, turns and looks down the hill. "What would happen to me if I went this way?"

"You would get lost, fall down and break a leg and then be eaten by slugs."

"I would eat them first."

"I wouldn't bet on it. I think they are faster than you."

"Careful, you are no young man either. You might get lost without a guide. And I am not talking about Michelle."

"You think I can't write a book about the theories of a silly Frenchie?"

Trading barbs works to energize us and soon we are at the top of the hill. We walk past the Tea Garden and take a wide paved path down the far side of the hill.

20: Task at Hand

"What took you so long?" says Michelle. "Did you get lost?"

"No, we just took the leisurely path."

"Follow me closely. We must hurry or we won't have time to see the Pittock Mansion." She leads us past a valley of small ponds fed by delicate waterfalls from the hillside. The ponds are surrounded by a ring of red and yellow maples and outlined by mounds of closely clipped azalea: a stunning display of the sculptural potential of nature. The gardeners have clustered the smallest mounds at the bottom of the gully along the stream edges and used larger single plants on the hillside to channel one's attention to the small churning stream that migrates through the green moss paradise.

"*Mademoiselle*, this is a gorgeous grotto of color."

"Take a moment to enjoy the tranquility, but we need to make our way toward Pittock Mansion. It will take forty-five minutes to walk there. That doesn't leave much time for a proper tour. We should be outside the gate and on the trail in the next twenty minutes," Michelle advises. "I suggest we enjoy this pond and then retrace our steps toward the entry."

Jean Baptiste and I nod our heads in agreement. Michelle holds us completely under her spell.

After obediently walking a bit farther, we return to the entry and find our guide waiting.

"Where do we go?" I ask.

"The trail starts just down the road."

Michelle leads off and walks about forty feet then turns to check on our progress. This becomes the pattern for the next hour.

Noticing a sign pointing up the hill, Jean Baptiste asks, "Are we looking for Wildwood Trail?

"Yes, follow the sign," Michelle says.

We head in the direction the sign points, turning uphill into the dark, heavy woods of Forest Park. The mature forest blocks all the direct sunlight except for thin sparkling beams among the tree trunks. Some trees are ladders for English ivy that scrambles up their craggy bark in a determined ascent to the forest crown and light. *I would like some of that light to warm me up.* Michelle adds her scarf to her ensemble and wraps her arms across her chest to conserve the heat gained in the sunny open garden.

After a tough uphill section of the trail, we reach an intersection with a sign pointing to the Pittock Mansion. We turn right and the path levels into a dirt ramp and winds in slow curves toward the top of the ridge. Although it appears we are traveling through an isolated deep mossy gully, our path is surrounded by homes just out of sight on the forest perimeter. Occasionally, the illusion is broken by the sound of a house-band practicing or the alien presence of a power pole stuck in the primeval grove. The ground here is covered with English ivy and menacing clumps of otherworldly ferns reaching out toward the open path to escape their crowded tenements.

After walking in silence for about twenty minutes, Jean Baptiste speaks. "We should discuss monetary policy in the book because that is what Keynes intended to promote. If we fail to address that policy head-on we sidestep his main point."

"That came out the blue."

"Not exactly, Pete. It came out of this dark and mysterious woods."

"I stand rectified on both points. I agree. We should have some commentary on the role of monetary policy. You know from my book, *Rule of Money*, I believe monetary policy is based on an improper understanding of money. Can I work that into our book?"

"Of course, the book should represent the best ideas, not just mine. I sought you out as a partner. It is about time we brought you onto the stage."

"Great. Let me outline what I would say. First of all, money is a concept of economics."

Jean Baptiste half-smiles. "In other words, you do not think money is a product of the state that it creates for our use."

"Correct, and because it is not a product, money is not subject to the rules of supply and demand."

"Interesting. Are you making a case that the market regulates the quantity of money? The market is where supply and demand rule over products, but not over items that are not products, such as money. So, the rules of supply and demand do not apply to money. Help me here, where does that lead?"

"If financial regulators throw off the chains of supply and demand theory, they are free to establish new rules to regulate how the money supply is increased or decreased."

"And what are those new rules?"

"Before I get into that, let me ask you a couple of questions. What's the purpose of government trade policy?"

A small smile moves across Jean Baptiste's lips as he considers his answer. "To help the consumer obtain foreign products, to help the businessman sell his products in foreign countries, and, I suppose, to help the economy avoid a trade deficit."

"In other words," I say, "to help the economy grow and prosper. Now, what is the purpose of government economic policy?"

"Oh, I see: to help the economy grow and prosper."

"Correct. So what should be the purpose of government monetary policy?"

"I have studied this topic thoroughly. My answer is: to help the economy grow and prosper."

Say returns to his roots: an economy begins with production, not with a purchase as Keynes argued. "Jean Baptiste, let me challenge you with a question about your own economic theory. What is the most significant policy a government can undertake to allow the economy grow and prosper?"

He breaks into a large smile and answers, "Develop the conditions for the formation of new business."

"Certainly low interest rates and a large money supply are part of the formula, but that is not all. The government needs to keep taxes as low as possible, reduce the cost and intrusive tendencies of the state, move the regulatory burden to business associations, ensure everyone who wants a job can get a job, make education free, eliminate special privileges for state employees, etc."

Michelle says, "That is very solid. That is the kind of wrap-up you need to end the book. Show readers that the solution is not some complex program, but a simple appreciation by monetary authorities of what their goal should be. Their proper goal is not world peace or an end to poverty, but fertilization of the job creating business sector.

"Confirmation of Say's idea that it's profit-making that drives the economy."

Michelle gives me a big hug, and then gives Jean Baptiste a peck on the cheek. I'm surprised she got that close to the tobacco machine. She must be genuinely excited.

As we continue up the trail, Michelle asks, "Have you two solved the employment problem Keynes' wrote his book to solve?"

I answer, "We replace more government with more business and get more jobs."

"Peter, can you do the mathematics to revise the IS/LM model to reflect what we have discussed the past couple of days?"

"I can. I will use risk in place of trying to earn a dollar on the back of employees as the controlling factor for economic growth."

"Jean Baptiste, how would following your theory have changed what the Federal Reserve did during the Great Depression?" asks Michelle.

"Ah, *Mademoiselle,* that is an intriguing question. One thing they could have done is protect inter-bank lending with insurance, because that lowers the risk of bank lending. Another thing that could have been done is..."

The patriarch of economics and his disciple walk up the trail beyond my hearing. He's done with his work. I am just beginning.

Other Books by Rand McGreal

Lost Foundation: Book One of the Lost Series, A Conversation with 18th century Economist Richard Cantillon

Credentials: Book Three of the Lost Series, An Economic Duel with Tao Zhugong founder of market economics in China during the 5th century BC.

Rule of Money: A Solution to the Global Debt Crisis

All are available at Amazon.com

Learn more about the New Market Economics

Blog: www.RandMcGreal.blogspot.com

Website: www.RandMcGreal.com